P9-DMQ-655

Form Follows Fiasco

Also by Peter Blake

The Master Builders — Le Corbusier, Mies van der Rohe, Frank Lloyd Wright

God's Own Junkyard
with R. C. Osborn

The Everlasting Cocktail Party: A Layman's Guide to Culture Climbing

Form Follows Fiasco

Why Modern Architecture Hasn't Worked

by
Peter Blake

An Atlantic Monthly Press Book
Little, Brown and Company
Boston/Toronto

COPYRIGHT © 1974, 1975, 1977 BY PETER BLAKE
ALL RIGHTS RESERVED. NO PART OF THIS BOOK MAY BE REPRODUCED IN ANY FORM OR BY ANY ELECTRONIC OR MECHANICAL MEANS INCLUDING INFORMATION STORAGE AND RETRIEVAL SYSTEMS WITHOUT PERMISSION IN WRITING FROM THE PUBLISHER, EXCEPT BY A REVIEWER WHO MAY QUOTE BRIEF PASSAGES IN A REVIEW.

FIRST EDITION
T 06/77

Portions of this book appeared, in slightly different form, in *The Atlantic*.

Library of Congress Cataloging in Publication Data

Blake, Peter, 1920-
Form follows fiasco.

"An Atlantic Monthly Press book."
Includes index.
1. Functionalism (Architecture). 2. Architecture, Modern — 20th century. I. Title.
NA682.F8B55 724.9 76-54801
ISBN 0-316-09940-6
ISBN 0-316-09939-2 pbk.

ATLANTIC–LITTLE, BROWN BOOKS
ARE PUBLISHED BY
LITTLE, BROWN AND COMPANY
IN ASSOCIATION WITH
THE ATLANTIC MONTHLY PRESS

Published simultaneously in Canada
by Little, Brown & Company (Canada) Limited

PRINTED IN THE UNITED STATES OF AMERICA

Designer: Samina Quraeshi
Design Assistant: Larry Yang

Contents

Preface

I never thought that I would write this book. I am a member in reasonably good standing of, roughly, the fourth generation of modern architects, doing what comes naturally to most of us: that is, designing and constructing modern buildings that owe almost everything to the inspiration supplied by the masters of the first and second generations in the Modern Movement. In 1960, I completed a book that eulogized three of those masters — Le Corbusier, Mies van der Rohe, and Frank Lloyd Wright — and so I was both publicly and privately committed to much modern dogma.

Then, a couple of years ago, Peter Davison, director of the Atlantic Monthly Press, came up with a suggestion that absolutely floored me: he suggested that the failures of the Modern Movement in architecture had been so massive that it was time for me to come clean — to confess and to offer alternatives.

Confess to what? Offer what alternatives? Trouble was obviously coming my way. The late Shadrach Woods, an architect and a good friend, had once said about Jane Jacobs's "revisionist" book on city planning, *The Death and Life of Great American Cities*, that "most of these writings, which have great popular appeal (like guidebooks on sex) propose only, in the end, to let popular misconceptions stand, to do nothing, and thus they are finally not only unproductive, but downright malignant." Shad, alas, was dead; but I could feel his critical eye on me, and I knew I had better be productive — or else!

This book is, of course, largely an indictment — of the glaring fallacies advanced by the Modern Movement, and of those who, like myself, swallowed and also promoted them whole. It began with an article in *The Atlantic Monthly*, in September 1974, which listed nine specific fallacies (as I perceived them), and then attempted to deal with each one. The article caused something of a stir in the architectural establishment in the United States and elsewhere (it was reprinted in several countries) and lost me most of my few remaining professional friends. (The American Institute of Architects, a delightful club whose officers are evidently a bit behind in their reading, awarded me its annual Architecture Critic's Medal a few months later, to the dismay of everybody else.)

One critic of my polemic wrote a well-researched letter to *The Atlantic Monthly* saying that I had inexcusably reversed myself over what I had professed some years earlier, and in public. This was a perceptive comment, I feel, since I had made it myself in introducing my scurrilous article. *Of course* I had reversed myself; *of course* it troubles me, to a degree; and *of course* I expect to stand corrected some day — but only if the facts correct me. Perhaps they will; but until they do, I think I should stick to the truth, as I perceive it today.

I am one of the few architecture critics in the United States and elsewhere who also designs and builds. I do not think that it is essential for architecture critics to know how to build — any more than it is essential for professional birdwatchers to know how to lay eggs — but it helps. I have designed and/or built about fifty modern buildings, and I like some of them to this day. I have also learned a great deal from designing and building them — an experience to which most architecture critics are not privy — and I challenge any of those who wish to challenge my facts. I do know a little whereof I write.

This book was read by a number of experts, including Stanley Abercrombie, a fellow architect and critic; Paul A. Donovan, an experienced construction materials analyst; and Richard L. Friedman, a real estate expert whose judgment I respect. I do not want to list all the others, for neither they, nor Messrs. Abercrombie, Donovan, or Friedman, were asked to endorse my conclusions; but I am most grateful to them — and they corrected some of my technical misconceptions just in time. It was also read by two or three friends, who advised me to burn it. It has not been read, so far, by my friend Seth McGovern, to whom it is dedicated — in the fervent hope that he will pass up my chosen profession.

In Hilaire Belloc's *Cautionary Verses* there is a tragic report on one Sarah Byng, a youthful enemy of literature, "who could not read and was tossed into a thorny hedge by a Bull," because she had failed to decipher the warning — BEWARE THE VERY FURIOUS BULL — planted at the edge of the field. I would like to rephrase Belloc's moral concerning Sarah Byng's misfortune:

Moreover she has wisely grown
Confirmed in her instinctive guess
That* architecture *breeds distress.

Peter Blake
Boston 1976

Introduction

I began to practice architecture around 1955, under a license issued, after certain tortuous examinations, by the State of New York. Like all of my contemporaries, I had been educated to accept a number of clear and idealistic precepts regarding architecture, planning, urban design, and related matters. Most of these precepts had been developed in Europe and in the United States between 1920 and 1950 by a handful of extraordinary pioneers whose visions dominated our lives, first as students and then as practitioners.

Five years later I began to realize that very little that my generation of architects had absorbed in and out of school made any particular sense. I, and many of my contemporaries, began to question almost everything: from the nature of buildings to the nature of cities (as these had been revealed to us); from the nature of the man-made world to the nature of nature itself. By 1960 or thereabouts, we confronted a severe crisis of confidence and competence. We knew that our beautiful diagrams had failed us, our clients, our art, and our time; but we had not, as yet, come up with any persuasive alternatives.

But I remembered that I had once heard a distinguished philosopher say that certain insights had come to him almost in a flash when he decided, just for the hell of it, to question every single assumption he had ever made, and to pretend, for a moment, that the exact opposite of that assumption might be true.

It turned out to be a marvelously liberating idea for me, as it apparently had been for him. I began to question much that I had been taught, as a student as well as a practitioner (and much of what I was then teaching), by simply assuming, for a moment, that the exact opposite might be true. Le Corbusier and others had persuaded us that there could be no civilization without cities — but that was before electronics produced a possible, partial alternative to face-to-face confrontation. Mies van der Rohe and others had persuaded us that the essence of modern buildings was "skin and bones" — the skin of glass, the bones of steel or concrete. But that was before interior climate became the most prominent (and most expensive) amenity in buildings, surely as entitled to architectural "expression" as the skin and bones. It was also before glass skins became recognized for the troublemakers they were and are, and before advanced structural engineers abolished the differentiation between skin and bones altogether! And Walter Gropius had persuaded us that the "building team" was the only realistic and competent entity for the creation of modern buildings; but somehow the buildings produced by such teams had turned out to be, quite often, among the less distinguished on our skylines. (Gropius had spent the first half of his enormously productive life in Europe, where the wonderfully American definition of a camel — "a horse designed by a committee" — was, presumably, unknown.)

I was not the only one, or even the first among American architects or critics, to question the validity of much modern doctrine. As early as 1968 Philip Johnson, probably the most intelligent architect America has produced since World War II, announced that "Modern Architecture is a flop . . . there is no question that our cities are uglier today than they were fifty years ago. . . ." James Stirling, the best British architect of the 1960s and 1970s, said at Yale University, in 1974, that he considered "ninety-nine percent of modern architecture to be boring, banal, and barren and usually disruptive and unharmonious when placed in older cities." And the Philadelphia architect Robert Venturi — the leading American "existentialist" designer of the 1970s — announced as early as 1966 that "architects can no longer afford to be intimidated by the puritanically moral language of orthodox Modern architecture. . . . Orthodox Modern architects have tended to recognize complexity insufficiently or inconsistently. . . . As participants in a revolutionary movement," Venturi continued, "they acclaimed the newness of modern functions, ignoring their complications."

Finally, in the fall of 1975, the Museum of Modern Art in Manhattan mounted a huge exhibition of the work produced during the nineteenth century at the École des Beaux-Arts in Paris — that hottest of all hotbeds of architectural reaction, that "public enemy number one" against whom the Modern Movement had battled for close to a hundred years, with the Modern Museum doing much of the battling for almost half that time! The implication was clear.

In short, many assumptions that I had held previously and firmly were shaken by others and began to disintegrate even before I myself began to doubt them. Other assumptions, needless to say, were confirmed. But, in any case, the exercise turned out to be rewarding: even where previous questions were confirmed, the confirmation was reassuring, for they had survived a fairly acid test.

This book is being written some fifteen years after my doubts first began to arise — fifteen years of writing about buildings and of building a few of them myself. It is a book of open questions about the man-made environment — questions that are usually not even asked, and should be; questions that are rarely answered, and will be, to the best of my ability.

1 Laboratory tower at Cornell University. Ducts and pipes have been "expressed" under a skin of brick.

1

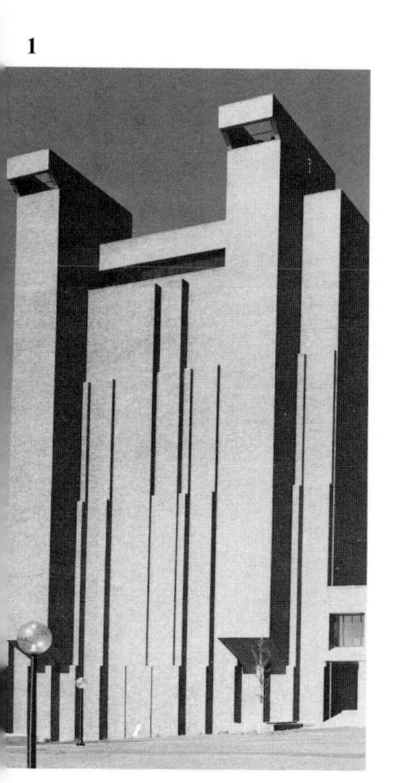

For, all around us, the environment we have built over the past century or so with supreme confidence is literally collapsing: the walls of our buildings are crumbling — literally; the well-intentioned zones mapped by our city planners are creating the worst ghettos in recorded history — literally; the best-planned schools by the world's most idealistic architects are producing a generation of zombies — literally; the finest public housing projects to be found anywhere in the world, and designed according to the noblest precepts, are turning into enclaves of murder, rape, mugging, and dope addiction, with the only way out a charge of dynamite to reduce those noble precepts to rubble — literally. Something or somebody, obviously, isn't quite up to snuff .somewhere up in the most exalted regions of our architectural establishment.

Not long ago Pierre Schneider, the French critic, said that the most radical, the most avant-garde position for an architect to take today was to refuse to build at all. A far cry indeed from Le Corbusier's dictum, only forty years ago, that the only alternative to revolution was architecture!

To question, to reexamine, to slaughter some of our sacred cows (and to perform autopsies long overdue) — that seems to be the prime purpose of this book.

The Fantasy of Function

The School of Architecture that I attended in the 1940s was located in a building believed to have been designed, some fifty years earlier, to house a school of dentistry. I cannot imagine what sort of a school of dentistry that pile of collegiate Gothic might have made: the acoustics were terrible, so that the shattering whine of dentists' drills would have reverberated endlessly through our vaulted halls. The natural (and artificial) lights were even worse — a fact that probably, and perhaps fatally, deflected the precise aim of those whining drills. The offices were dingy, the corridors infested with spittoons and papered with a green plastic mold, and the stairs steep and slippery. It was a building of such stupefying squalor as to make any self-respecting, would-be dentist want to switch to something like preventive sanitation.

Yet in spite of all of this, and perhaps because of it, the School of Architecture at the University of Pennsylvania was a marvelous place in which to be a student.

It was, for one thing, a great building against which to rebel. It was, for another, a building capable of absorbing great globs of paint and India ink and rubber cement and paper pulp without any loss of architectural aplomb. In fact, the accretions of filth that had been contributed by generations of rebellious students had added a certain patina that improved, rather than detracted from, the ambience of this gloomy pile of bricks.

A dozen years or so later Paul Rudolph — unquestionably one of the best architects of his generation and of mine — completed the new School of Art and Architecture at Yale. It was and is an extraordinary building, perhaps *the* building of the 1960s in America. It revealed in overall composition and in every detail the pervasive influence of Frank Lloyd Wright and of Le Corbusier upon Rudolph's time. Its spatial organization on twenty-eight distinctly different levels was enormously subtle, and its play with light, texture, and form was dazzling. There was not a single detail, however small, that had not been studied by its architect with tender, loving care. And six years after Paul Rudolph's brilliant School of Art and Architecture was dedicated, its students attempted to burn it to the ground.

This appalling act of vandalism seems to suggest several things about the state of Yale, as well as about the state of modern architecture. It suggests, first, that Yale students in the later 1960s were slobs or worse; and it suggests, second, that they were idiots, since the building was most solidly and most visibly constructed of reinforced concrete, a material that does not burn terrifically well.

But aside from this evidence of the decline and fall of Yale's behavioral and intellectual patterns, the decline, if not the fall, of Paul Rudolph's brilliant structure is evidence of something else — or seems to be. It appears to be material evidence in the divorce that has been proceeding, for some time, between form and function.

Nobody is quite certain who first proclaimed that "form follows function." Most historians think it was Horatio Greenough, and all agree that Louis Sullivan, the master architect of the American skyscraper of the late nineteenth and early twentieth century, made it his slogan, though not, entirely, his guideline. As Marcel Breuer once put it, "Sullivan did not eat his functionalism quite as hot as he cooked it!" In any event, "Form follows function" — or Functionalism — did become *the* dogma of the Modern Movement from its inception. And what the examples of Paul Rudolph's building at Yale and that dingy ex–school of dentistry at Penn seem to suggest, in tandem, is that form not only does not necessarily follow function, but that it may, in fact, be the mortal enemy of the latter.

2

2 Yale's School of Art and Architecture. A complex form containing complex spaces — each tailored to a specific function.

3 Yale's School of Art and Architecture in the process of being defaced by its students.

For Rudolph's building had been defaced and viciously brutalized long before some playful Yalies, evidently under the influence of a badly needed agent to broaden their limited perceptions, tried to set fire to the place. It had also been effectively rebuilt by those students: the spacious, two-story drafting rooms had been subdivided into little plywood shacks — student favellas — which totally demolished the intended uplift of the halls but apparently served the students better, or so they thought. The roughly hewn concrete walls had been covered with singularly unimaginative graffiti, and the floors had been randomly pissed upon, or imprinted with chewing gum and cigarette butts. As for the students in the so-called allied arts — painters, sculptors, photographers, etc. — they had long complained of the total inadequacy of their accommodations; Rudolph had, in fact, confessed to some of his friends that he did not, strictly speaking, consider these artists to be allies.

Since that day of the Great Yale Conflagration, when those tons of reinforced concrete refused to ignite, the university's management has further vandalized the building. Like all bureaucracies, the Yale management is enamored of orderliness and troubled by poetry. And so the School of Art and Architecture has now been converted into wall-to-wall, floor-to-ceiling secretarial pools. Only ten years after its dedication, it has been recycled into a file cabinet.

Yet in Rudolph's original building the spirit of architecture, and the very real genius of its architect, were everywhere. And they remain, despite the gang-bang. For somehow the building continues to defy its assailants. It has a tough and rather tragic beauty, battered but almost unbowed. Yet there is no question at all that the building has been deeply hurt — and so has its architect. He did not visit it until five years after that fire. And he will not visit it now that the university's management has finished it off.

4 New School of Architecture at the University of Pennsylvania faces Frank Furness's ornate extravaganza. The spirit of architecture seems to have been lost.

4

Meanwhile, down at the University of Pennsylvania, the former brick Hall of Denture is doing just fine. Remodeled a dozen times by successive generations of more or less irreverent occupants, the place works just as badly now as it ever did, and just as cheerfully. In 1968 the university's powers-that-be decided to build a brand-new concrete, glass, and brick school of architecture — in a style best described as department-of-sanitation modern — next to the marvelous old Furness Building, completed in 1890 by the architect after whom it was subsequently named. Frank Furness's modern neighbor has proved to be an almost unmitigated disaster in functional as well as in aesthetic terms. And the old Hall of Denture, now abandoned by its hapless architecture students, underwent still another metamorphosis: it now houses the university's Geology Department with the same frowsy insouciance with which it previously embraced its architects and its dentists. Nobody — or almost nobody — has the remotest idea of who designed it in the *first* place, and nobody — or almost nobody — cares enough to have tried to find out. (It was, in fact and for the record, one Edgar V. Seeler; he left his one, solitary mark on the university's campus — and in the hearts of many generations of students — and, having designed and built his Hall of Denture, Edgar V. Seeler retreated into obscurity.)

5 Baltimore's Mount Royal Station remodeled into a College of Art.

6 Nineteenth-century malthouse in Suffolk, England, converted into a concert hall.

7 Nineteenth-century courthouse in Manhattan converted into a library.

8 1854 public library in New York City converted into an experimental theater.

The example of these two buildings is not an isolated case, not by any means. All over the world, buildings that have been recycled from an earlier function to a new one seem to serve their users better today than they ever did before — and better than contemporary, brand-new efforts designed and constructed to a form that supposedly follows and expresses its function.

The best museums in Italy and in Spain, for example, tend to be recycled convents or palazzi of the Renaissance or of the Middle Ages, whereas modern museums, designed specifically to display and celebrate the art of our century, look like cut-rate department stores with bargain basements up to the roofline. In Great Britain, the best concert hall may be a recycled brewery — now known as the Maltings at Snape in Suffolk; in Baltimore, the best art school may be a recycled railroad station — the Mount Royal Station, now become the Maryland Institute, College of Art; in New York, the best library may be a recycled courthouse — and the best theater may be a recycled library! In San Francisco, the nicest shopping center, Ghirardelli Square, is a recycled chocolate factory; in St. Louis, the beautiful headquarters of an educational laboratory was carved out of an abandoned Civil War hospital; and in London, one of the nicest office buildings may well be a recycled warehouse.

5

7

6

8

9 **Richardsonian police station in Boston converted into the Institute of Contemporary Art.**

10 **Fifteenth-century Castello Sforzesco, in Milan, converted in 1954 into a Museum of Antique Art.**

9

And as the cost of *new* construction has become almost astronomical in the developed countries, the recycling of *old* buildings is becoming more and more attractive — in economic as well as philosophical terms. In Salt Lake City, Utah, for example, a charming new shopping center was created within the abandoned vaults of the former trolley-car barns, and the center is an economic success as well as an aesthetic one. In Italy, many palazzi of Renaissance vintage have been almost routinely recycled into museums: in Palermo, the fifteenth-century Palazzo Abbatellis is now (as of 1954) the National Gallery of Sicily, thanks to the architect Carlo Scarpa; in Milan, the Castello Sforzesco was turned into a dazzling museum by the architects Belgiojoso, Peressutti, and Rogers some ten years later; and in Verona, Carlo Scarpa recycled the fourteenth-century Castelvecchio into a very modern museum — in concept, not in content — at about the same time.

In the United States there have been some moves in the same direction. One of the best "modern museums" in Boston, for example, is the Institute of Contemporary Art, housed in a nineteenth-century, Richardsonian ex-police station that used to contain forty "drunk tanks." Its namesake in London, on The Mall, is located in a space carved out of John Nash's 1827 Carlton House Terrace; it works exceedingly well, except for the occasionally confusing fact that all sequential exhibitions must be hung to read from right to left because the configuration of the narrow and deep space forces circulation counterclockwise!

These recycled structures are not isolated events. For several years, the modern Milan architect Giancarlo de Carlo has been recycling certain structures in Urbino bequeathed to us by that extraordinary Duke of Urbino, Federico da Montefeltro, most notably a convent that de Carlo converted into a library for the law school of Urbino's famous university. In Boston, if you have any sense at all, the best place to live is not on Beacon Hill, but in one of those early nineteenth-century wharf buildings, almost solid granite, and recycled in the early 1970s by architect Carl Koch. In an unlikely place called Imlayston, New Jersey, ninety minutes from Manhattan, the landscape architect Robert Zion has his office inside a 1695 mill building that he recycled when the local authorities decided to condemn it and threatened to tear it down. It is not only an extraordinarily efficient office, it is also one of the most beautiful spaces occupied by any professional in the United States. And finally, near

11, 12 The Scarlioni Room; and a view of the Elephant Arcade in Milan's remodeled Castello Sforzesco.

11

12

Modena, Italy, the Pio Castle (A.D. 1000, or thereabouts) is now the most moving modern war memorial anywhere in the world — again, thanks to the genius of the architects who converted the Castello Sforzesco.

These architects — Scarpa, Belgiojoso, Peressutti, Rogers, de Carlo, Koch, and Zion — are not musty preservationists; they are among the farthest-out avant-gardists of the second half of this century. They are the direct descendants of the early functionalists, and they are demonstrating, through their own, often inspired, work, that Form has, in fact, taken leave of Function.

Some modern architects have not been entirely unaware of this rather disturbing evidence. Many of the best of them, in fact, live *not* in modern houses of the kind that they might prescribe for their clients, but in old shacks and warehouses and lofts that they have managed to bend and twist into a new form and space. Mies van der Rohe, Eero Saarinen, James Stirling, and many more, lived or continue to live in buildings not at all designed originally to accommodate their special needs.

The architect most clearly aware of the problem — of the impending divorce of Form from Function — was the late Mies van der Rohe. He was, in fact, deeply troubled by it, and his concept of "universal space" — that is, a structure capable of accepting almost any kind of function, from city hall to automobile showroom — continues to be an interesting notion and is explored in many different areas of building.

The concept is simple: since future functions are clearly unpredictable today, our buildings should be designed so flexibly that they will be able to accommodate — and indeed, to welcome — all conceivable functions in years and generations to come. In simplistic terms, this means that our buildings should be vast lofts, without interference from columns or from vertical plumbing lines and ducts, within which anything from a school to a factory to a theater could be constructed at some unpredictable, future time.

This is an eminently reasonable idea, at least on the surface. Slightly below the surface, however, there are a couple of time bombs, not inconceivably planted there by that wonderfully gentle radical, Mies van der Rohe himself. Time Bomb No. 1 is the effect upon the free enterprise system, which flourishes through the accelerated obsolescence of buildings as much as of automobiles. Making buildings obsolescenceproof is, quite clearly, a subversive attack upon the American system, since our tax policies have encouraged accelerated depreciation and thus rapid disintegration and replacement of buildings — all in the name of "making work." A "universal space," adaptable to a wide variety of uses, suggests an alternative to the periodic demolition of buildings that will not please those with a vested interest in such demolition. Time Bomb No. 2 is the demonstrable fact that infinitely *flexible* buildings tend to be incredibly expensive to construct — and may, in fact, not work anywhere near as well as *inflexible* buildings. It is not inconceivable that a building could be designed and built to function as a place of worship on Sundays, and then to convert — by pushing buttons — into a house of ill repute during the week. But the mechanical gadgetry and trickery required to achieve this interesting transformation would probably cost at least two or three times as much as building two separate houses, side by side — one of God, the other of Satan — with one open when the other is closed. (Janitorial services could, presumably, be shared, as could the heating.)

The impact upon the free enterprise system of Mies van der Rohe's "universal space" theory is minor. As the free entrepreneurs become more aware of what ails their system, the notion of accelerated depreciation is beginning to trouble them as much as it troubles their fellow men and women — that is, the consumers. It is quite obvious, even to the manufacturers of aluminum curtain walls and steel girders, that they and we can no longer hope to produce as much cubage as we (and they) need to accommodate a six- or eight-billion population, and so the idea of a building capable of being recycled for a future, unpredictable use no longer seems to be the threat to the free enterprise system that it once was.

But the notion of a multipurpose building — not advanced solely by Mies van der Rohe — is something else again.

Two types of building, in particular, have been designed and constructed in recent years to be totally flexible. The first is the completely flexible, infinitely changeable theater; the second is a similarly flexible and changeable laboratory or research hospital.

The leading pioneer in the design of flexible theaters is George Izenour, whose projects include facilities in which floors, ceilings, performance and acting areas can be altered and even interchanged, literally, by the push of a button. Multipurpose theaters of the kind long advocated by Izenour have been constructed in considerable numbers in Europe, especially in Germany — Cologne, Gelsenkirchen, Ulm, and elsewhere. But one gathers that the enormous costs involved have begun to sour German theater technologists on the idea; it seems more practical, and more desirable, to build several single-purpose theaters (possibly side by side within one large complex, or scattered throughout the community), rather than one expensive multipurpose hall that might end up costing more than all the required single-purpose halls put together (and, of course, accommodating a much smaller audience on any given evening). Moreover, it is really very difficult to design a hall that will serve both the dance (with its need of a very wide stage and, probably, a very wide proscenium) and, let us say, a puppet show. It can be done; but most of the time the result will be an inferior facility at both ends of the scale. The multipurpose theater, in other words, is an interesting intellectual concept that tends to produce a number of rather inferior single-purpose facilities, no two or three of which can be used simultaneously, and all of which may well be housed more economically in several single-purpose halls designed and built to more exacting and particular specifications. (There are occasional exceptions: the multipurpose casino in Montreux, Switzerland, can be converted into a two-thousand-seat concert hall that is acoustically near-perfect. But *most* multipurpose structures for the performing arts tend to perform inadequately for most, if not all, of their intended functions.)

Mies van der Rohe's "universal space" theory doesn't fare much better in the design of modern laboratories or hospitals. To make a laboratory or a hospital totally flexible and receptive to every imaginable (but really unpredictable) future requirement, it is necessary to build vast spaces without interior columns, and interstitial floors (between the usable floors) to house every conceivable duct, wire, pipe, or other mechanical device. It *can* be done, and it has been done, specifically by the late Louis Kahn in his Salk Laboratories, at La Jolla, California, and by the designers of hospitals like the McMaster Medical Center in Hamilton, Ontario, and similar hospitals in Minneapolis and New York. It can be done, but only at enormous cost. When it is done, the result is indeed a virtuoso achievement, admired by all except those who have to foot the bills (e.g., taxpayers, patients, and the rest). The open, columnless floors permit future generations to shift partitions at will and to create spaces of almost any desired size, shape, and function. And the interstitial floors, crammed with esoteric piping, tubing, wiring, and ducting, permit future generations of maintenance men to poke wires and ducts and pipes up or down into the floors above or below to serve any need in any given location at any given moment.

13 Diagrammatic section through a new health center in Brooklyn, N.Y. Walkable interstitial floors contain all electro-mechanical systems, leaving the hospital floors completely flexible in plan.

13

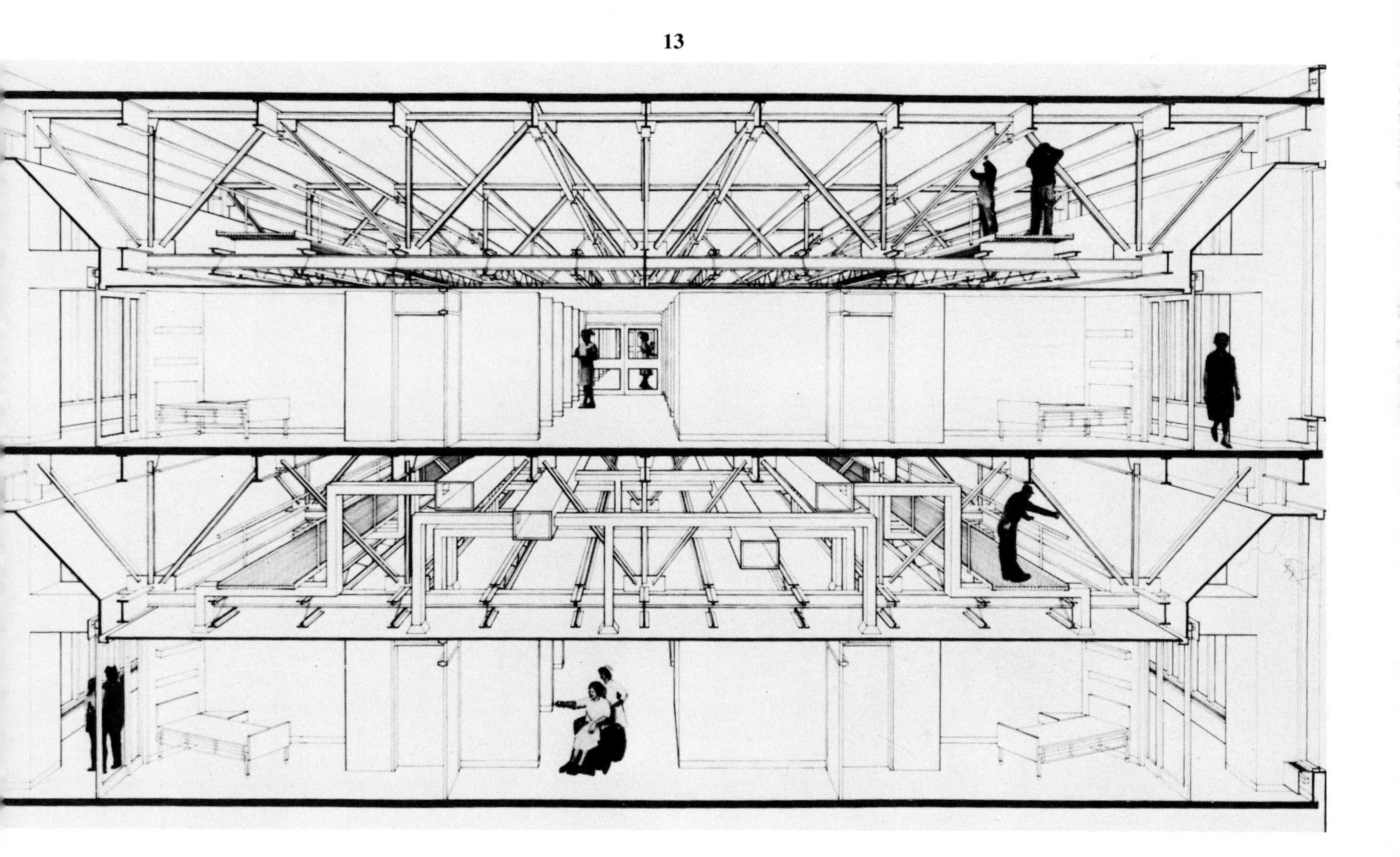

It is, indeed, an intriguing idea, and I don't wish to debunk it. But I wonder if anyone in his right mind working in the area of transportation technology, say, would seriously consider designing a vehicle that could roll, swim, and fly with equal ease. Obviously, it can be done, but such a universal transporter would be vastly expensive to produce and of limited value.

A universal space, infinitely flexible, may in fact turn out to be antithetical to human creativity. I once worked with a brilliant theater designer, David Hays, on a project for an "ideal" experimental theater. He was very polite, but the idea clearly did not thrill him. To him the most challenging, the most stimulating theater up to that time was the original Circle in the Square, on Sheridan Square in New York's Greenwich Village. He took me to see the place. It was a dingy basement with an untrustworthy ceiling approximately seven feet above a floor slab that inspired even less confidence. The space was cluttered with temporary cast-iron columns scattered about in critical places to jack up the ceiling. It seemed just about the worst kind of space in which to perform anything — a play or, for that matter, a wake. And yet Hays and his associates found the endless awkwardnesses with which this space was so liberally endowed to be challenges and inspirations not likely to be found in a perfectly attuned universal space. And out of this first dingy Circle in the Square grew the Off-Broadway theater — the most creative new development in the performing arts in twentieth-century America. A perfectly flexible universal space might not have stifled that development, but it was clearly not indispensable to it.

"Form follows function," in short, is not the sine qua non of modern architecture. Much of the time, form is nothing more than an educated guess about function. Much of the time, for better (but probably for worse) form follows the mortgage interest rate. Much of the time, form in modern architecture is antifunctional. Much of the time, this may be all to the good.

The Fantasy of the Open Plan

14 Modern house in the Japanese tradition. The plan is entirely open, and spaces are separated by sliding screens.

14

No single technical innovation has been more directly responsible for the development of modern architecture than the invention of reinforced-concrete and steel framing. What differentiates these structural systems from conventional masonry and from most conventional wood construction is this: in most traditional building systems, the walls carry all the loads of floors and roofs above; quite obviously, the load-bearing walls cannot be moved without causing instant collapse of the superstructure. Once the walls have been constructed in a given alignment, the spaces created by them are fixed in width, length, and height: only door openings can connect adjoining spaces. (Some structural systems, primarily those employed in temples, churches, and other spaces of assembly, use arches and vaults between masonry columns; but except in such buildings, the determinant of spaces is the bearing wall, and the resulting spaces are finite and clearly circumscribed.)

What differentiates modern concrete and steel construction from bearing-wall construction is that the supporting structure that holds up floors and roofs above can, in concrete and steel, consist of a very few slender columns spaced widely apart. The resulting interior spaces can be defined by non-load-bearing screens, often of very ephemeral materials; massive walls, as such, are no longer necessary to hold up buildings.

Frank Lloyd Wright was one of the first architects to understand the implications of strong, delicate column and beam structures. What these made possible, in his view, was the "open plan": a succession of spaces that could merge into one another, often without door separations, and lightly insulated from one another by screens of opaque or possibly translucent or transparent materials. Both Le Corbusier and Mies van der Rohe adopted Wright's notions of the "open plan" and of "open space" and, if anything, carried his notions even further: the one-room house, or the one-room apartment, became an aesthetic triumph that every modern architect sought to achieve. Kitchens were opened to dining areas, dining areas to living areas, living areas to studies or libraries, libraries to playrooms. Only bedrooms and bathrooms generally (but not always) retained a degree of privacy.

Wright's philosophical concept of open spaces flowing into each other and separated by screens came out of the traditions of Japanese architecture, out of both the simplest Japanese house and the most elaborate palace, like Katsura.

What Wright and his successors in Europe and the United States failed to realize was that the "open plan" as developed in Japan depended for its success *entirely* upon one or both of two factors: the availability of cheap servants and/or the availability of enslaved wives.

No traditional Japanese "open plan" house could possibly function without the ubiquitous but generally invisible servant and/or wife who kept the pristine spaces in immaculate order by stashing away all the messy appurtenances that might offend the eyes of her husband or his male visitors. She stashed them away (together, presumably, with the children) in special areas outside the immaculate open plan; and she spent a good part of her time seeing to it that the elegant open spaces remained presentable.

It is amusing (at least to some male critics) that two or three generations of architects ostensibly wedded to concepts of human freedom and equality should base most of their planning principles upon a way of life quite unthinkable without human slavery! Yet this is precisely true: today, as Japanese women are beginning to reach out for and attain equal status, the traditional house has become increasingly unacceptable even in Japan. When a Japanese architect today builds what looks like a traditional house, you may be certain that there are very solid doors separating the living and sleeping areas, and that as much weight is given to privacy as to the delicate, aesthetic balance of open spaces that work only for families in which the husband is more equal than anybody else.

15 Exhibition House by Mies van der Rohe, constructed in 1931, in Berlin. The plan is as open as that of any traditional Japanese house.

16 Interior of Katsura Palace, in Kyoto (bottom).

15

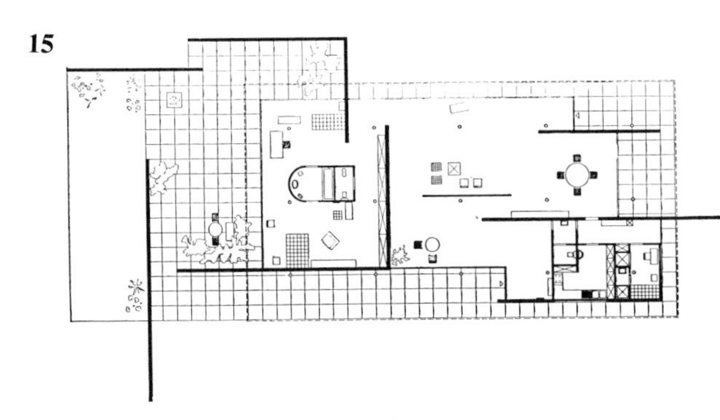

16

Yet, in the Western world, the open plan is still very much in vogue. Every day avant-garde architects plan houses and apartments in which parents will madden each other and children will grow up psychotic. Apartments are designed and built (often in response to governmental planning regulations) in which splendid and generous living-dining areas are backed up by strings of minimal bedrooms intended to house families of up to eight or ten — in arrangements manageable only if the slave-wife is employed to keep the splendid living spaces immaculately presentable and the backroom kids chloroformed so as not to annoy Daddy and his pals.

Architects around the world continue to admire Le Corbusier's 1952 Unité d'Habitation at Marseilles, and rightly so, but for the wrong reason: it is a spectacular hunk of sculpture — and a terrible hunk of living space. It is a huge slab of concrete some 450 feet long, 200 feet tall, and nearly 70 feet thick; it contains close to 340 apartments that house something like 1,600 people; there are fifteen floors of apartments, and a two-story "shopping street" that runs the length of the building about a third of the way up. The huge concrete monolith is supported on a double row of concrete struts and topped by a marvelously plastic roof garden complete with playgrounds, a restaurant, a movie theater, and much, much more. The Unité, in short, is a vast and stunning piece of concrete sculpture (and an assemblage of many smaller but equally stunning pieces of concrete sculpture); but as an assemblage of dwelling units attuned to the needs of twentieth-century living in plan, section, elevation, or general spatial organization, the Unité is a farce.

Its apartments lack all pretense of privacy: its children's bedrooms are, in effect, sliding-door closets, about six feet deep; there are no places in which children can escape their parents, or vice versa. The only place for either to go, to get away from it all, is out. Le Corbusier's apartments are, without doubt, masterpieces of volumetric virtuosity. Unhappily, they are also destructive of all family life. (Le Corbusier and his wife had no children.)

Wherever the pattern of open apartment planning has been followed in major housing complexes, the result has been predictable: children, refusing to be cooped up and deprived of their own privacy (and hence freedom), have congregated in public spaces and vandalized them. At Pruitt-Igoe, the St. Louis housing project that became so hopelessly crime-infested that it finally had to be dynamited only two dozen years after its completion, the architects actually provided wide-open communal spaces — generous landings on each floor — so that kids could escape whenever life became intolerable at home! They could and did, and proceeded to use those spaces as battlefields on which to ambush the neighbors.

Open planning has, in recent years, been applied to the design of office areas as well. So-called modular partition systems were designed to offer infinite flexibility in the partitioning of office floors. The idea was that these partitions could be rearranged in a jiffy anytime a newly appointed first vice-president required a more splendid office to reflect his increased status.

That, at least, was the theory. In fact, these infinitely flexible partitions tended to be infinitely inflexible and infinitely more expensive than routine, fixed partitions of block and plaster. The flexible partitions tended (on the exceedingly rare occasions when they would, in fact, be pushed around) to cause havoc with air-conditioning, lighting, wiring, and, occasionally, plumbing arrangements. And, most important, being ephemeral, they transmitted the irritating sounds of typewriters, adding machines, teletypes, and telephones to neighbors near and far.

The designers of infinitely flexible modular partitioning systems for offices — systems that had been revealed to us through the principle of the open plan — had little trouble finding solutions to overcome the dramatic failings of the basic idea. To take care of the absence of acoustic privacy, they inserted expensive noisemakers (or ''white'' noise) in the air-conditioning ducts on the rather bizarre theory that one way of getting acoustic privacy was to generate so violent a racket that nobody could hear anybody talk or, for that matter, think — as, for example, in a New York City subway train. Next, to make sure the air-conditioning would work even after the flexible partitions had been moved from here to there, the designers developed complex localized controls that enabled each square foot of space to obtain the precise degree of heat, cold, humidity, or dryness required by that square foot's occupant. Similarly complex and enormously costly controls and service systems were developed to make lighting, wiring, and telephone services also infinitely flexible. And so the cost of office buildings soared: infinite flexibility, once touted as the ultimate economy for an unpredictable future, began to cost so much as to make that future predictably unattainable! Meanwhile, nobody paid much attention to the boring idea of simply building buildings with nice, solid offices in them — offices that were quiet, private, and properly heated or cooled — and letting *people* move from one office into the next in the course of their corporate ascent as part of that exhilarating experience.

As in many other areas of human ingenuity, the idea of infinite modular flexibility soon acquired a powerful constituency of vested interests: manufacturers of infinitely flexible modular office partitions sprang up on every continent and effectively silenced any expressions of doubt — at least in professional journals — that might have gnawed away at their highly profitable operations. Still, by the end of the 1960s the game was up: anybody who had ever worked in (or managed) an office constructed of infinitely flexible modular partitions knew that flexibility was vastly more expensive than inflexibility — and that it was also, in most cases, vastly more inflexible. It took far more time (and money) to move those infinitely flexible partitions around on their modular grid than to persuade a second vice-president to move into the former first vice-president's quarters, and it usually messed up everything in sight — ceiling systems, carpeting, air-conditioning, wiring, and telephone outlets, to mention only a few.

The manufacturers of all those modular panel systems were not about to throw in the towel. Instead, they came up with still another version of the open plan: why not do away with everything in the way of partitions and just put everybody into one great big bullpen?

Well, ''bullpen'' is not the sort of term that is likely to turn on a corporate client or his employees, and so a new term had to be coined. A German firm of cybernetically conditioned social psychologists came up with the term *Bürolandschaft*, or ''office landscape.''

An ''office landscape'' is a great big bullpen with little partitions about chest-high that make oddly shaped alcoves in which people can sit and work and from which they can't see a window. The plan of an ''office landscape'' looks like a labyrinth in an amusement park, and it works quite well in one or two respects. The acoustics are no worse than they are in a modular office because you can still put those subway noises into the air-conditioning ducts, and the lighting and air-conditioning work a little better. There is a lot of social interaction, because occupants of various alcoves can stroll about and have bull sessions with occupants of other alcoves, and there is a great deal more social democracy, because the boss occupies the alcove right in the middle of the ''office landscape,'' so that *everybody* is scared to open his or her mouth — not just the people next door.

An ''office landscape'' is also supposed to promote a more uninhibited exchange of profound ideas. Judging by a recent sampling of ideas exchanged by the occupants of a spectacular ''office landscape'' near Tacoma, Washington, designers of such open spaces might find the occupants' reactions instructive — and discouraging — or at least those reactions audible above the artificial (or ''white'') noises emanating from the air-conditioning ducts.

17 Mies van der Rohe's 1930 Tugendhat House in Brno, Czechoslovakia. It is so "universal" a space that it now functions quite well as a gymnasium for handicapped children.

18 Bird's-eye view of a typical "office landscape" layout.

17

18

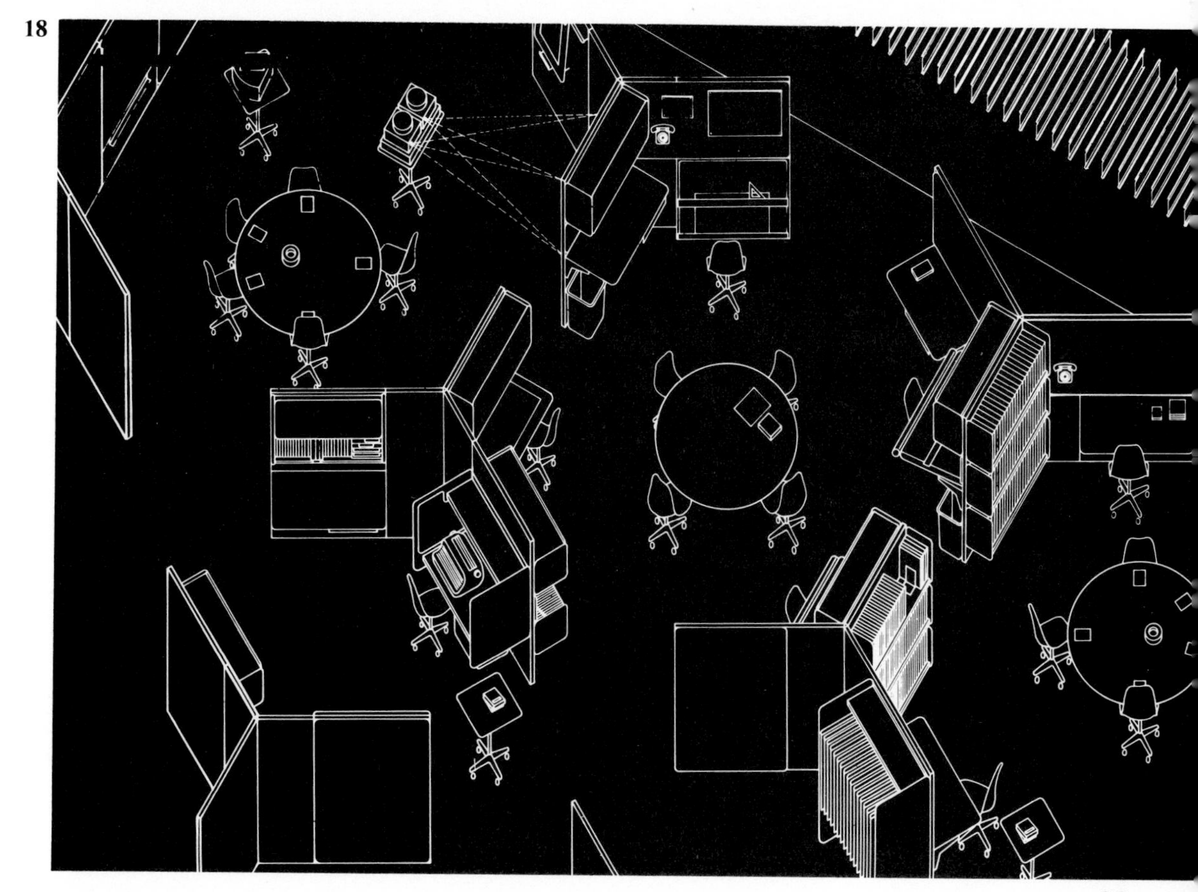

For the trouble with "office landscape" planning is that it provides even less privacy than the now standard modular system. It is also incredibly wasteful of space, because the square footage required by all those flow patterns of circulation that separate all those islands or alcoves of work space may be two or three times that required by conventional corridors.

Wasting space is, of course, one of the great luxuries that architecture can provide — at least to the rich and to the rulers of enslaved societies. The open plan — that most "free" of all modern dogmas — was, as we have seen, copied from the authoritarian traditions of Japan. Professor Jennifer Taylor, the Australian architectural historian, has said, "In large [Japanese] establishments, such as the homes of the prosperous, temples and palaces, the visitor is surprised to find one empty space followed by another, and another, and another. These are not the well-known multipurpose rooms of the small house, but reception rooms, audience chambers and prayer halls. . . . They exist simply as places for honor, peace and delight."

Of course. And no one even remotely touched by the magic of architecture would wish to live in a world without surprise. But enough is enough. Most modern architects have their own offices in old buildings with massive walls of brick and stone, and with windows that open and doors that close. Some of the most exciting architectural offices in Europe are located in remodeled monasteries or convents or castles, not in sealed, air-conditioned, glass and metal towers, modularly subdivided and openly planned. Some of the most significant modern architectural ideas — such as those promulgated by Serge Chermayeff and Christopher Alexander — have juxtaposed community with privacy, or the open plan with the monastic cell. The former, a device for democratic interaction; the latter, a retreat for self-fulfillment. It is curious, surely, that the masters of the Modern Movement took their guidelines for an architecture of community from an extremely autocratic social order, and that they denied — and continue to deny — retreats for self-fulfillment to those for whom they design open plans.

In their beautiful and romantic masonry caverns, the finest architects in Europe and North and South America are busy designing office buildings with infinitely flexible modular office spaces created by wafer-thin partitions, or with "office landscapes" illuminated by unreal light and ventilated by equally unreal air.

Few of the architects ever move into one of their own ephemeral creations. They know what is best for them — places with solid walls, solid doors, and real windows that let in real air and real light. The open plan is for somebody else, preferably someone who is deaf to noise, blind to views, and equipped with his or her own portable supply of air.

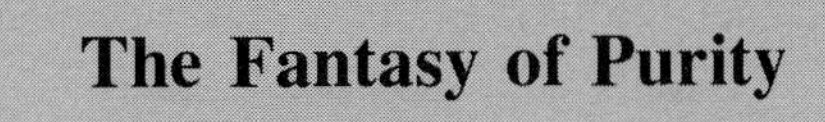

The Fantasy of Purity

19 Constantin Brancusi's "Marble Fish," in the sculpture gallery of The Museum of Modern Art.

19

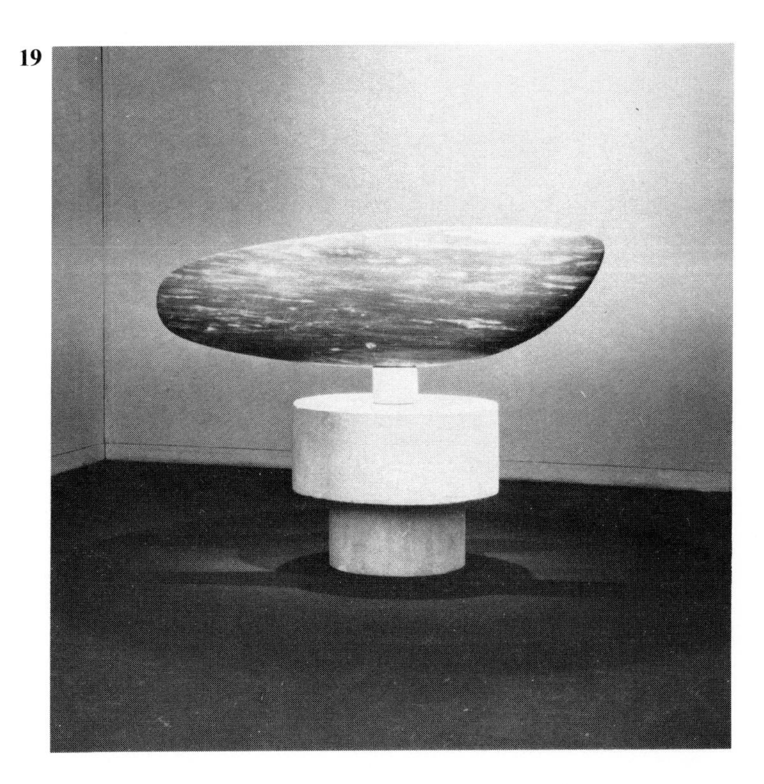

Ornament und Verbrechen is the title of an article published by the Viennese architect Adolf Loos, in 1910. The implication was, quite clearly, that ornament was and is a crime. Even the most straitlaced American Puritans must have been slightly discombobulated: they had long known that plainness was a virtue — but ornament a *crime*? Come off it, Loos — a frivolity perhaps, or a naughtiness. But a crime? And so defined by, of all people, a *Viennese*? This had to be a put-on.

It wasn't. Not only has ornament been a crime in modern architecture ever since Loos issued his pronunciamento, but the converse — that unadorned Puritan plainness is the supreme virtue — has been one of the guiding principles of the Modern Movement for most of this century.

Unadorned Puritan plainness can, of course, be a very beautiful thing — and a very sensuous thing, too. Brancusi's marble *Fish* is an object of almost unmatched beauty (as well as unmatched sexiness), and one feels that there are not very many works of twentieth-century sculpture that even remotely approach the perfection of that sliver of stone.

But Brancusi's *Fish* stands inside the galleries of New York's Museum of Modern Art — air-conditioned, humidity-controlled, feather-dusted, and properly guarded. It stands in the unreal world of one of the century's most thoroughly sanitized emporia. Brancusi used to keep his sculptures in his Paris studio shrouded in cheesecloth, explaining to visitors that "it makes them nervous to be seen or touched." In the Museum *The Fish* is almost as far removed from the real world as when Brancusi shrouded it.

20, 21 Poured-in-place concrete under different conditions of weathering and weather.

20

21

The architecture about which Adolf Loos wrote — and to which he contributed so much — is, however, part and parcel of the real world. And the real world treats unadorned Puritan plainness with a certain amount of disdain: it cracks it, stains it, rusts it, buckles it, delaminates it, and rots it. The real world of ice and snow and hail and rain and broiling sun and soot and otherwise polluted air is not a respecter of unadorned Puritan plainness. Indeed, Brancusi's *Fish* might have turned into marble dust if it had been exposed to the real world for any appreciable length of time.

The facts of life in the real world have taken a terrible toll of many of the most distinguished buildings of the Modern Movement. The earliest buildings of the International Style were constructed of seemingly perfect, seemingly machine-made slabs of opaque, translucent, or transparent materials, all joined along precise, razor-edged lines, all determined to convey a cool and rational approach to industrialized building.

And they looked convincing, especially in diagrams, and in photographs taken immediately after the ribbon was cut and properly retouched to emphasize the sheer and perfect flatness of the slabs, the hairline precision of the razor edges.

In fact, however, these great monuments of the Modern Movement were usually built of terra-cotta blocks covered with stucco — the former a material in common use for at least five hundred years, the latter in even commoner use roughly since the beginning of time. In 1932, when Henry-Russell Hitchcock and Philip Johnson published their influential *The International Style*, they pointed out that "brick is often covered with stucco even by [modern] architects who claim to be uninfluenced by aesthetic considerations . . . the use of [exposed] brick tends to give a picturesqueness which is at variance with the fundamental character of the modern style." What, then, is the answer? Hitchcock and Johnson, like most other theorists and practitioners of the Modern Movement, looked to a new material: "a material like stucco, but elastic and with a wide color range

22 Precast concrete curtain wall, with typical streaks of soot and other discoloration.

23 Self-oxidizing steel curtain wall, after two years of routine exposure.

22

23

. . . would be ideal.'' Unless such a new material were found, they implied, the Modern Movement would be in trouble.

To achieve the machine-made look deemed essential by the Modern Movement, there had to be seemingly mass-produced building components as well. And so the finely edged, industrial-looking windows and doors of those same great monuments of the Modern Movement were painstakingly handcrafted (in the name of ''honesty,'' no less!) by cabinetmakers or ironworkers; and the lovely, Machine Art hardware justly celebrated by the Museum of Modern Art and others (also for its ''honesty'') was just as painstakingly handcrafted by jewelers and other latter-day medieval craftsmen.

The composite result — at least in photographs — did indeed suggest a new world of industrial forms of the sort that Walter Gropius was searching for at the Bauhaus. And it is entirely reasonable to assume that then, as now, prototypes of such new products had to be handmade.

But the underlying premise of building in the International Style — the premise of sheerness, flatness, smoothness, unornamented plainness — remains, to this day, an impossible dream. Impossible, for the simple reason that the facts of building in the real, outdoor world — the facts of such mundane problems as weathering and maintenance — make it virtually impossible to attain the ideal of a flawless architecture of pure, geometric forms.

Nobody knew this better than Le Corbusier, who, after a quarter-century flirtation with pure forms, turned after World War II to what became known as the New Brutalism — a building vocabulary of deliberately rugged, deliberately crude and imprecise surfaces and forms. Indeed, some of Le Corbusier's New Brutalist structures — especially the Palace of Justice at Chandigarh, capital of the (then) East Punjab — are so crude in execution as to call into question the professional competence of whoever was supervising the construction.

24 Board-formed concrete — or the return to handicrafts.

24

Although Le Corbusier's New Brutalism had a major impact on architects around the globe, the dominant theme in most modern architecture continues to be precision — sleekness, plainness, unadorned flatness, razor-edged sharpness. All very nice — but all very, very difficult and very, very expensive to achieve in the real world of building, and all even more difficult to maintain over the years, as weather and wear-and-tear take their toll.

It is a fact of life recently discovered by a well-advertised group of architects known as the New York Five, who have been busy resurrecting the early (and later disowned) work of Le Corbusier, with its intended hard-edged whiteness. They, like Le Corbusier, have found it exceedingly difficult to build a large, precise, dead-flat wall of almost any modern material that will not cause endless problems. Exposed, flat, poured-in-place concrete surfaces will frequently stain and develop shrinkage cracks — and are almost sure to look prison-grim under overcast skies (whereas brick or stone can look quite beautiful even in a rainstorm). Concrete, after such a rainstorm, will display great "sweaty hatband stains," in the words of the British Modernist James Stirling, who has been trying, for some time, to imprint diagonal striations on his concrete walls in order to direct the predictable rivulets of soot into reasonably acceptable patterns. Stirling's striations are either precast into his concrete slabs or created by the formwork that shapes his cast-in-place concrete. When texture is applied to concrete walls after they have hardened — by so-called bush-hammering, for example — the bush-hammering machines will probably bite into the concrete unevenly: more deeply at the top of a concrete pour, less deeply at its bottom, where the aggregate (i.e., the pebbles, etc.) tends to settle while the concrete is still semiliquid. (This can be avoided by several exceedingly expensive methods — such as injecting cement into the aggregate — by which time the finished wall may cost only slightly more, per square foot, than platinum.)

25, 26, 27 Machine Art, fifteen years later. Although neglect obviously took its toll, no comparable toll would have been exacted from tried and tested conventional materials.

25

26

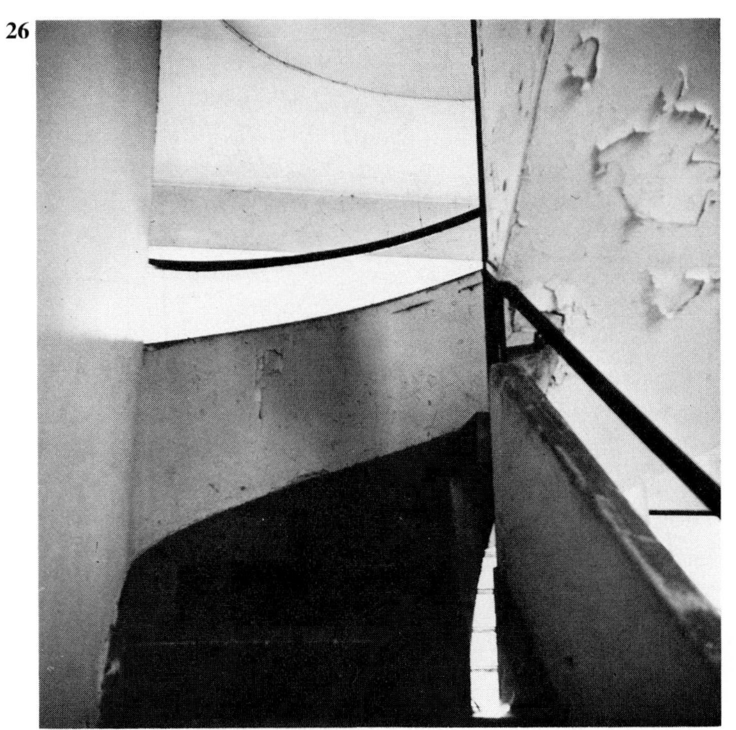

27

It is possible, of course, to build a large, precise, and roughly dead-flat wall of precast concrete, but in many U.S. cities such precast units have to be installed by stonemasons (under union regulations), so the cost is once again quite excessive, and the quality of color and light and texture really does not approach that of more traditional materials.

As for dead-flat walls of metal, these have an annoying tendency to "oilcan" — that is, to lose their dead-flatness as the heat of the sun and the cold of night alternately expand and contract the neatly machined surfaces — unless they were fabricated of very heavy gauge material or elaborately reinforced internally. And this is not merely an annoying characteristic of modern panel materials. When the new annex to Washington's National Gallery was designed, with a dead-flat wall of marble veneer several hundred feet long, it was found that the expansion and contraction of the marble, under heat and cold, would tend to squeeze out the flexible mastic that would have to be used to fill the joints between the marble slabs, and that the mastic would then begin to drip and stain the smooth marble façade indelibly. Only by inventing a complex neoprene gasket with which to fill the joints could the architects maintain the flatness of those hundreds of feet of blank marble wall.

In the original National Gallery building, completed in 1941 by John Russell Pope, the same sort of marble was used — but the wide expansion joints that were needed were easily concealed in that neoclassical building behind applied pilasters and other ornament. The intriguing fact is that *the entire design* of the beautiful modern addition, created by I. M. Pei some thirty years later, depended for its success upon the absolutely smooth anonymity of that long façade; so the design was, in effect, saved by the invention of that complex little neoprene gasket! Most modern architects have not been quite so inventive, nor quite so fortunate: smooth planes are drawn and detailed on paper, but when they are translated into a real building something deplorable may (and often does) happen to the smoothness and the plane.

One of the problems has been that the U.S. building industry (and the building industries of other nations) has failed to do its homework adequately to support the aspirations of the Modern Movement. "Research," in the building industry vocabulary of the United States, in particular, really means little more than inventing an aluminum shingle that looks like a cedar shingle, but costs less; or, possibly, inventing a cedar shingle that looks like one of aluminum, but won't "oilcan." Most "research," in other words, is the search for bigger and more profitable markets — not the search for better products. Innumerable modern architects have been seriously hurt in lawsuits because they have trusted products that their supporting industry manufactured and wildly promoted without having given them much supportive research: plastics that discolor and crack, sealants that dry up or "bleed," self-oxidizing steel that stains every other material in sight — and continues to rust, even though the manufacturer says it won't, and innumerable other materials and gadgets tailored to the whims of the Modern Movement that fail to perform when the chips are down.

One of the reasons modern architects continue to be misled by the manufacturers of many of the new miracle products is that the professional magazines do not dare to report the failures. When they do, their advertisers — the manufacturers of many of those shoddy materials and products — will gang up on the offending publication and wipe it off the map by, in effect, blackballing it. Or by blackballing the editor who dared to tell the truth. When I was in charge of a fairly prominent and professional U.S. publication on architecture and related matters, I had the nerve to mention — not in my own magazine, but in *The Atlantic Monthly* — that glass was not necessarily the building material it had always been cracked up to be. Whereupon one of the two or three principal glass manufacturers in the United States withdrew his advertising from my professional publication and apparently induced other potential advertisers to do the same: a very effective form of censorship, since my own publication was thereby put out of business, despite a growing and hugely enthusiastic readership. *The Atlantic* was, presumably, put merely on notice. The lesson was not lost upon other architectural magazines, which have since steered clear of subjects that might offend the tender sensibilities of their advertisers — if, indeed, they ever did want to offend those sensibilities.

28 Thirteenth-century brickwork at Albi, surviving the test of time.

28

This sort of censorship is not, of course, limited to the building industry. One must assume that any medical journal that tells the truth about the abrasive effects of aspirin upon human plumbing might have trouble attracting advertisements from the manufacturers of that miracle drug. But in the building industry, and in the professional publications that prosper or survive only if and when the manufacturers of building products buy advertising in them, the situation is especially venal. The professional publication is not merely expected to suppress all critical evaluation of the performance of any advertised miracle product; it is expected to devote page after editorial page to uncritical reviews of the shoddiest "new products" sloughed off onto the market by the manufacturers of the latest sort of supergook, guaranteed to permit walls to expand and contract like rubber bands, and guaranteed to fail not a moment before the planet Earth turns into a pumpkin. And when the supergook fails to fulfill its advertised expectations (long after the manufacturer has fled the scene or gone out of business), the poor, credulous modern architect is left holding the bag. His dogma had told him that modern technology was on the verge of breaking through to supergook, and when the breakthrough was, at long last, proclaimed, he or she seized upon supergook, and accepted it on Bauhaus faith.

It would be ridiculous, of course, to blame the dubious practices of many manufacturers of building products on the Modern Movement. But it does not seem unfair to point out that the Modern Movement wrote some very precise specifications for what it wanted the modern building industry to produce. It specified that there should be assembly-line precision, that there should be smooth, impervious finishes, and that there should be the capability of making vast expanses of impeccably sleek sheets of entirely new materials — metals, plastics, composition boards — all impervious to heat, cold, rain, or snow, all dimensionally stable (so that no wide expansion joints would mar the vast sweep of any wall), all light in weight and inexpensive to mass-produce.

29 Brooklyn Heights street scene — a return to traditional forms and traditional materials.

Well, the millennium may be just around the bend, but it isn't with us yet. The product specifications explicitly or implicitly written by the International Style have so far proved utterly impossible to fulfill. After all, the performance of many building materials is profoundly affected by such immutable factors as the weather, and that, in a way, has been getting worse rather than better. The man-made weather, in cities especially, now contains such ingredients as smoke, soot, airborne gases, asbestos flakes, acids, and poisonous fumes, none of which existed to any appreciable degree in the days when Palladio built with stone. So even our traditional building materials are being subjected to increasingly severe tests — and some have started to flunk them. Our new materials, often inadequately tested before being rushed to the marketplace, have a very long way to go. Most of them, judging by their initial performance, will never make it.

There has been something close to a conspiracy of silence in this matter, because the leading architects of the Modern Movement are quite conscious of the fact that if the technological underpinnings of the dogma collapse, then much of the dogma itself may soon follow suit. Yet in every developed country in the world the leading architects have quietly retreated from those visions of never-never land: James Stirling, in Britain, builds increasingly with brick; the late Alvar Aalto, in Finland — who is posthumously emerging as one of the most important (and most underestimated) pioneers of the Modern Movement — returned, after World War II, to brick, tile, marble, and bronze. Ulrich Franzen, Romaldo Giurgola, Victor Lundy, and others in the United States now finish many of their buildings in brick and other traditional materials rather than with one of those miracle products that seem invariably to invite disaster. The few important architects who still attempt to build with miracle materials, and according to orthodox modern dogma, are just as invariably threatened with lawsuits and, subsequently, faced with bankruptcy.

In 1924 Mies van der Rohe, an architect who really did know how to build in the real world (he had been trained as an apprentice to his father, who was a stonemason) wrote this about building technology and its relationship to the Modern Movement: "The industrialization of building methods [is] the key problem for architects and builders. Once we succeed in this, our social, economic, technical *and even artistic problems* will be easy to solve. . . . The nature of the building process will not change as long as we employ essentially the same [traditional] building materials, for they require hand labor. . . . *Our first consideration must be to find a new building material.* Our technologists must and will succeed in inventing a material which can be industrially manufactured and processed and which will be weatherproof, soundproof, and insulating. It must be a light material which not only permits but requires industrial production. . . . Then the new architecture will come into its own." [Italics added.]

What Mies van der Rohe was saying is that the new architecture could *only* come into its own if industry provided an entirely new range of building materials — plain, smooth, hard-edged, pure, precise, and impervious to just about everything. He was saying, in effect, that unless modern industry came up with such miracle materials, modern architecture was sunk. Judging by what has happened over the fifty years or so since he wrote his specifications, he may have been right.

This is a profoundly disturbing conclusion. In many disciplines, researchers and other innovators will state a premise, and then subject that premise to the acid test of experimentation. The premise is an educated hunch; if subsequent tests prove that the hunch was right, the researcher wins a Nobel prize; if the hunch is proved wrong, the researcher goes off on another tack or takes up a new profession.

In the discipline of modern architecture, a great many hunches were postulated in the first couple of decades of this century — and a great many of them have proved to be mistaken. None has proved more mistaken than the hunch that industry might invent "a new building material" that would enable us to write a new, pure, plain, and precise language of vision. Yet, despite the highly visible failures all around us, the researchers of the Modern Movement have clung stubbornly to propositions that have clearly been invalidated by the facts of life in the real world. More important, perhaps, modern architects have shown precious little interest in the results of exhaustive and controlled laboratory tests, even when they were available. Most Modernists, it seems, were bewitched by their own myths: they wanted to believe in miracles, because the pioneers had told them that it would take a miracle for the new architecture to come into its own.

The Fantasy of Technology

30 Petrochemical installation in Sicily. Such symbols of modern technology — often far removed from the real world of real buildings — continue to dominate modern architecture.

From its inception in the mid-nineteenth century, the Modern Movement was preoccupied with the urge to catch up with the Industrial Revolution. The preoccupation became an obsession: technology — modern technology — and all its images began to represent the one article of faith upon which the Modern Movement either stood or fell.

To understand how profoundly modern faiths depended upon modern technology for their sustenance, one needs only turn to the Soviet Union. There we find an almost religious obsession with the *symbols* of modern technology: the skylines of Soviet cities are dotted with tall cranes (rather reminiscent of the work of Tatlin and other "Russian Constructivists" of earlier years) — the icons of the future — all busy lifting precast, prestressed, prefinished reinforced-concrete elements into their preordained positions. It does not matter to the authorities that there are, in fact, millions of skilled hands in the Soviet Union ready and willing to build handcrafted buildings, and to do it exceedingly well; all that matters is that prefabrication, precasting, prestressing, and prefinishing are, clearly, the wave of the future! The Modern Movement is as inconceivable without modern technology as Christianity is without the cross.

This article of faith is not without its logical foundation. The Industrial Revolution had replaced the handcrafting of singly made objects with the mass production of large numbers of identical objects. (It had also introduced mechanization in many other areas, of course — mining, agriculture, transportation, and so on — in which the final "product" was not a standardized, mass-produced object at all, but rather a commodity, a raw material, or a service. But in architecture the greatest need appeared to be the mass production of buildings, or of building components that could be assembled rapidly to satisfy the needs of a fast-growing population.)

Initially, these efforts to mechanize, standardize, and mass-produce architecture got off to a promising start. James Bogardus, for example, a remarkable American inventor, patented a system for the construction of buildings made up of standardized panels of cast iron and glass as early as 1849, and some of his earliest efforts in curtain-wall prefabrication still stand in Lower Manhattan. These cast-iron and glass façades by Bogardus and his many imitators are as "all glass" as Manhattan's Seagram Building, completed by Mies van der Rohe a hundred years later. Only in certain, relatively insignificant details does the wall of the Seagram Building represent a technological advance over the work of earlier pioneers, Bogardus and many others.

For, in fact, very little has happened since the mid-nineteenth century to advance that most admirable and desirable of architectural ideals — the industrialization of building.

It has not been for lack of trying. The architects of the so-called International Style — especially Walter Gropius, Le Corbusier, and their innumerable followers in Europe and elsewhere between the two world wars — were literally obsessed with the idea of some sort of modular building system. Walls, floors, roofs, partitions, and all the rest would be prefabricated, under controlled conditions, on the assembly lines of modern factories, then shipped to whatever site was in need of these precisely machined, modular units; and finally snapped or bolted or zipped together in a jiffy to form neatly finished houses or apartment blocks, or schools, factories, offices, and so forth, each of them a monument to rational building and to the cool art of the machine.

The idea was that buildings could thus be produced rapidly enough to keep up with population growth; that on-site labor time could be reduced to an absolute minimum because such labor was inherently inefficient (being adversely affected by poor weather, and by the patent difficulty of a worker using precision tools while perched, for example, on a tall scaffold swaying in the wind); and, finally, that the qualities of finish, inside and out, that so distinguished other mass-produced objects (like automobiles) could begin to distinguish buildings as well. (A further objective was to create modular building types that could be unsnapped, unbolted, and unzipped just as easily as they had been initially assembled — on the theory that future generations might wish to add to, or subtract from, their buildings, or even disassemble them and move them to another site.)

None of these objectives has been attained to date.

Instead, in the United States and other developed nations, idealistic and adventurous souls who have gone into prefabrication — or "systems building," as it is now known, presumably to wipe out all memories of earlier disasters with "prefabrication" — have gone into bankruptcy in droves. Indeed, the building industries around the world are littered with the graveyards of heroic would-be prefabricators — and, incidentally, their equally heroic public and private backers — who believed in all the theories and were demolished by all the facts. More than a hundred years after James Bogardus, just about the only U.S. building products really prefabricated in standard, modular units or sizes are bricks and sticks. Rolled-steel sections (I-shaped, H-shaped, L-, Z-, T-, or U-shaped) are indeed prefabricated — in several hundred "standard" sizes (a contradiction in terms, of course); and so are some windows, some doors, some pipes, and also light bulbs. All of these "standard" building products are manufactured in hundreds of different sizes, materials, colors, finishes, and weights, which makes them about as "standard" (and interchangeable) as ink-blots.

31, 32 Typical prefabricated cast-iron and glass façades, assembled in Lower Manhattan during the second half of the nineteenth century.

31

32

33, 34 Precast concrete boxes sit on a site in Montreal, waiting to be assembled into ''Habitat.''

33

34

It is virtually impossible today to assemble a building of any sort in the United States out of large modular assemblies routinely available on the market without introducing innumerable ''special details'' or ''special components'' that instantly increase the cost to a point above that of a comparable, conventionally built structure. In 1970, a $3 million rehabilitation center I designed for the Mental Hygiene authorities in New York State was completed at a cost well below the amount budgeted. It was a ''modern'' building in every respect — except in respect to technology. Everything in that rather sizable building (with the exception of a few plastic skylights and a number of essential mechanical services) could have been constructed close to a hundred years earlier — and better (because craftsmen were much more skillful then). Had I designed this building to be technologically ''modern'' as well — an assemblage of factory-made components — it would have exceeded the assigned budget by 25 to 50 percent, and the client would have been sued by the taxpayers for squandering our hard-earned dollars on some harebrained experiment that had never shown much promise of ultimate success.

My own limited experience is not an isolated example by any means. It is a simple fact, rarely admitted by all those who are ideologically or financially committed to current systems of ''industrialized building,'' that prefabricated developments, from Habitat in Montreal to Thamesmead outside London, have almost invariably cost much, much more to build than comparable, conventionally built structures.

Diagrammatic perspective of California's SCSD construction system. A wealth of special details contradicted the designers' stated intentions to standardize.

36 Brick, block, concrete and glass building completed, in 1972, in New York State. Most of it could have been built a hundred years earlier.

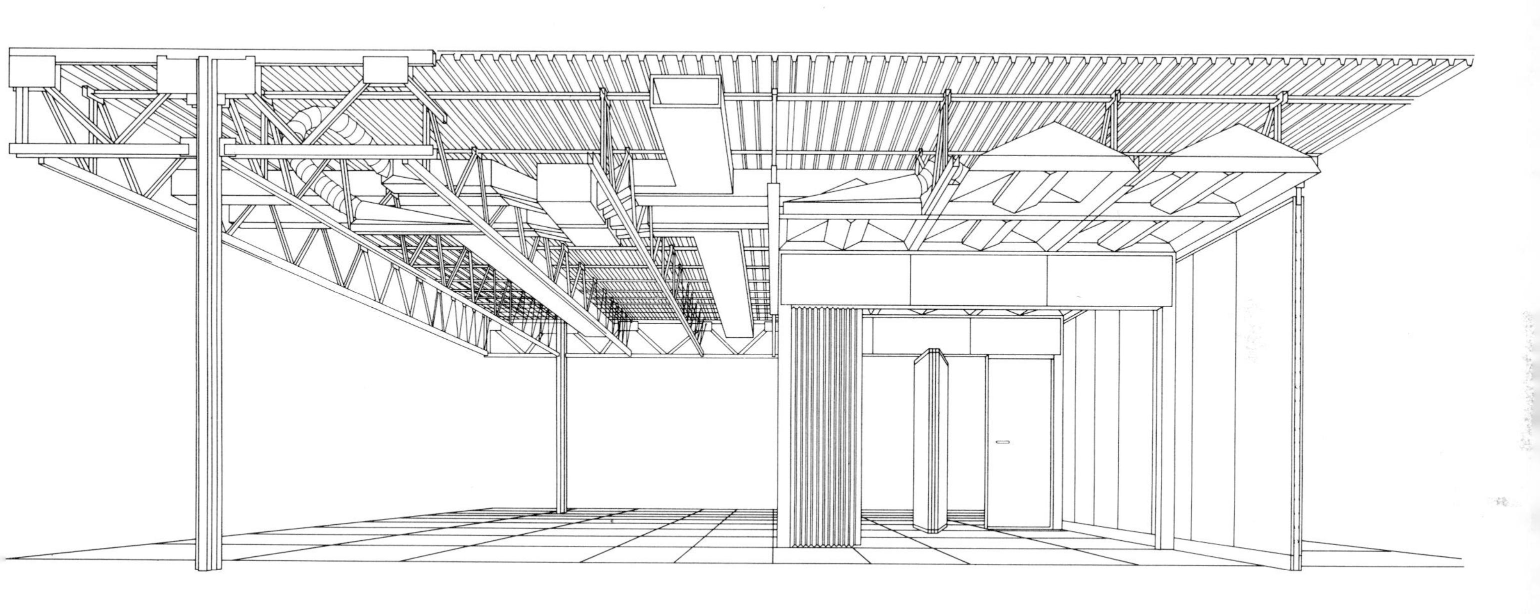

The claims to the contrary made almost daily by sophisticated critics (as well as by less sophisticated journalists) are almost invariably false and tend to perpetuate some dangerous myths. Charles Jencks, a highly perceptive historian, wrote in 1973, in his book *Modern Movements in Architecture*, that the celebrated Schools Construction System Development, or SCSD, "became both successful in California and influential throughout the world. In California," Jencks continued, "at least thirteen schools [were] built with it by 1966, at substantial savings, and thousands of entrepreneurs had appropriated the [SCSD] sub-systems for their own particular requirements." With all due respect for Jencks and the creators of the SCSD system, this statement is untrue. As for journalistic fantasies, in 1974 *Time* magazine stated that Moshe Safdie, the energetic builder of Habitat in Montreal, had "built a second Habitat as a low-income housing development in Puerto Rico." Safdie deserves all the credit in the world for having *realized* Habitat in 1967 (for good designers of such projects are a dime a dozen, but performance is what really counts in the end). Safdie performed energetically, even incredibly, in Montreal. Still, the "builders" of that second Habitat, in Puerto Rico, might convincingly dispute the claim that their project was either low-income or low-cost or, in fact, completed at all. The Puerto Rican project was indeed started, but it had to be abandoned halfway through construction because it proved to be technically and economically unbuildable. At this writing, the site is an abandoned wasteland, dotted with the ruins of technological dreams.

Other public claims usually cite Buckminster Fuller's geodesic dome as superman's gift to ordinary men in the area of industrialized housing. Fuller, a man of great integrity, never made such claims. His own most significant experiments in the field of housing had to do with the prefabrication of service units — a truly brilliant insight, offered by Fuller as early as the 1930s, while everybody else was still preoccupied with houses of cards, or with equally unstable "panel systems." Still, hardly a day passes without some chanted eulogy to the geodesic dome as the cure-all of the modern world.

Even some of Fuller's intrepid backers — those who survive in the flesh as well as those in the chips — are not unanimously enchanted with the economics of their experiments. Fuller's prototypes have invariably cost more to produce than their conventional equivalents; but, then, prototypes invariably do, and Fuller's were, at least, rational as well as poetic. Other prototypes by other, less intelligent innovators were neither. Not only their prototypes, but also their stereotypes, tended or promised to be outrageously expensive, and they further tended or promised to take much longer to complete than their conventional equivalents. That, of course, was really the final straw: speed of construction had always been the one irrefutable justification advanced by proponents of prefabrication when every other argument failed.

In Nairobi, Kenya, to cite an example, the United Nations Environmental Program (UNEP) — a UN agency slated to become something on a par with UNESCO — determined in early 1975 to build about 120,000 square feet of office space, and in very short order. UNEP officials went to the three established prefabrication firms in Kenya and asked them to submit bids on the project. None was willing or able to tackle the job: not one could guarantee the time schedule, and not one could guarantee the equally tight budget.

But the UNEP headquarters *were* built — not in six months, as originally planned, but in five and a half — and they were built, handsomely, for just under the established budget. They were designed and built by two young Kenyan architects who were thoroughly familiar with the real world of building — and somewhat disdainful of the world of architectural and technological theory. They used conventional, traditional building methods, and they used them well.

This dichotomy between the real world and the world of modern fantasy is really deplorable; for mankind's need for housing and for other forms of shelter is more desperate than ever, and the building industries of the developed countries are falling further and further behind in their feeble efforts to meet those needs. In the United States alone, for example, President Johnson and the Congress determined, in 1968, that the nation must have 2.5 million new housing units annually for the subsequent ten years in order to meet its basic needs. In fact, the United States has rarely attained more than 60 percent of that modest goal since. Much of the reason for that failure must be ascribed to the inhumanity of a subsequent administration, but some of it is unquestionably the fault of a building industry that has failed miserably to fulfill the mission so clearly spelled out by American and European pioneers of the past hundred and fifty years.

37, 38 Abandoned Habitat project in Puerto Rico.

37

38

There are several reasons for the monumental failure of true prefabrication in the United States. The most obvious ones are these:

First, there cannot be any true prefabrication of building components unless and until a nation's building industry agrees to adhere rigorously to a set of dimensional and qualitative standards (including, for example, the metric system, which the U.S. building industry strongly opposes). In a free society, in which manufacturers of building components (and of everything else) are free to concentrate on clobbering the competition rather than on collaborating with it, the tendency is for each manufacturer to establish his own standards to be as different as possible from his competitors'. Manufacturers of kitchen appliances, for example, make a point of dimensioning their wares so that they cannot possibly be used in conjunction with those of any other manufacturer; they further defeat industrywide standardization by coloring their appliances so that they will not match those of the competition, even in the neutral shade of white.

The reason, of course, is that each manufacturer wants his customers to use his, and only his, products. (The resulting dimensional and qualitative hodgepodge has a similarly absurd side effect: it makes it virtually impossible to standardize and prefabricate plumbing stacks, whose connections must be aligned with the center lines of the plumbing fixtures they serve. To understand the full absurdity of this particular aspect of our free enterprise system, one might consider what would happen if each manufacturer of automobile tires were to determine his own dimensional standards, thus forcing automobile manufacturers to supply different axles to fit different wheels and tires. In short, it is highly unlikely that dimensional and qualitative standardization, without which true prefabrication is unthinkable, can be impressed upon today's U.S. building industry — either by persuasion or by legislation.

Second, the mass production of large building components can occur only where there is mass consumption, i.e., a smooth and even flow of distribution. This means that dealerships similar to those established by General Motors and others must be set up around the country, with their own warehousing and financing facilities, so that the manufacturing plant can be assured of a steady demand — which, in turn, will keep its assembly lines rolling at top efficiency.

Unfortunately, no such distribution networks have been set up to date, and it is doubtful that they can be, given the innumerable special requirements of local building codes and of different climatic conditions across the North American continent. We do have some sort of national building code — but it can never be a uniform code, applicable equally to Alaska and Florida. To return once again to the automobile analogy: it is as if General Motors were forced to meet hundreds of different and conflicting safety regulations in manufacturing its cars for hundreds of different markets. The economies inherent in mass production would vanish overnight.

Third, the very size of the United States creates severe problems of economical mass distribution. Most manufacturers of prefabricated houses today — those who are still plodding along, motivated by some inexorable death wish — have found that they cannot compete in price with the locally and conventionally built product beyond a radius of about 150 miles from their manufacturing plant. This means that each manufacturing plant is severely limited in the size of its potential market, and therefore severely limited in the efficiency and economy of its assembly-line operation. Prefabrication plants, like other plants, can only become efficient and competitive when the volume of their production approaches their maximum capacity. But if the market is limited in size and fragmented by conflicting local requirements, such plants will rarely come even close to reaching their maximum capacity, or to turning out a product that can compete with the locally and conventionally built equivalent.

Fourth, the highly individualistic character of a free enterprise society such as ours seems to resist standardization at every turn. Henry Ford may have said, about his Model T, that "they can have it in any color so long as it's black"; but Mr. Ford's heirs seem to have found the market for black cars somewhat limited outside the confines of the mortuary trade. Although Americans do, in fact, lead lives shaped very largely by identical, standardized products and services, they prefer to think that they do not: the early, post–World War II houses in that vast subdivision, Levittown, have been so radically altered by their inhabitants by the addition of porches, dormers, bedroom wings, and various curlicues that the original standardized shell is now unrecognizable.

So there is a very real resistance to standardization in a free society, and the resistance is not limited to the consumer by any means. It is very widely shared by some of the producers as well, specifically by the building trades unions, many of which have fought prefabrication, tooth and nail, ever since they decided it would threaten the livelihoods of their members. Although the national and international headquarters of some unions have long paid lip service to the idea of mass-produced construction, local unions almost everywhere continue to resist the idea in principle as well as in practice. Shortly after the end of World War II, an enterprising manufacturer decided to mass-produce a so-called service core: a complete "package" containing kitchen, bathroom, and utility room, with all fixtures, pipes, ducts, and wires in place, ready to be plonked down in any typical suburban house.

The first twenty of these beautifully designed and beautifully made "packages" arrived on a site near Detroit; local union plumbers and electricians promptly refused to install them. Finally, after nine months of heated debate (during which the units, parked on a sidewalk, were exposed to weather and vandalism), the local unions agreed to handle the "packages" — by disassembling them on the sidewalk and then reassembling them, piece by piece, in each of the houses. The manufacturer, needless to say, thereupon went out of business.

Union obstructionism is a little more sophisticated now. In New York City it is impossible to install a very well designed and well engineered modular ceiling "package" in office buildings because the powerful local unions have insisted that the installation, a very rapid and simple process, must be attended by one electrician, one sheet-metal worker, and one plumber — in addition to the mechanic needed to snap the ceiling "package" into place. The resulting installation (which contains all lights, ducts, sprinklers, and acoustic panels) thus costs almost twice as much as a conventionally assembled ceiling system of comparable design. And other examples of similar obstructionism, designed quite deliberately to defeat prefabrication, are legion.

Finally, there is one further reason for the pitiful failure of prefabrication in the United States to date, and it is the result of certain historical twists and turns.

The notion of modular standardization — many building panels of identical size, joined together in a jiffy on the site — was largely of European origin. The modular panel and the magic joint were pursued singlemindedly by European pioneers, and the notion was brought to the United States when these innovators arrived just before World War II.

The notion made considerable sense for European (and, of course, Japanese) conditions: on-site labor was cheap, so the on-site assembly of a vast assortment of prefabricated panels presented no serious economic problems. But building materials were expensive, so the prefabrication of different building panels, with its attendant paring-down of wasted metals, plastics, and so on, on the assembly line, promised some significant overall savings.

In the United States the exact reverse is true: labor is relatively expensive and materials are relatively cheap. Quite often a building will be designed in the United States to use identically dimensioned steel or concrete columns and beams, and other identically dimensioned pipes, ducts, and cables, simply because identical dimensioning facilitates and thus reduces the cost of on-site labor — and this may substantially offset additional costs of materials that have been, quite deliberately, overdimensioned. The United States is, of course, built on waste, but not, generally speaking, on wasted motions.

39, 40 **"Imaginary elements . . . related in any way at all to an assumed raster system," according to its designer. "They may rest on it, stand apart from it at a constant distance, or occupy an eccentrically disposed, rhythmically repetitive space." Translation: a prefabricated house.**

41, 42 Not a Chinese puzzle, but an ingenious connector system intended to replace the common nail.

So the basic principle of the panelized building, constructed of great quantities of identical modular units, all joined together (on the building site) along literally miles of seams that had to be made weathertight — this principle simply did not apply. Many wonderfully inventive designers spent decades, if not lifetimes, trying to perfect *the* absolutely perfect, universal joint — the magic mechanical device that would join their modular panels together in wedlock (yet leaving open the possibility of some future disengagement, for the sake of greater postmarital flexibility).

But it was all in vain. The universal joints, the seams, the gaskets, the unbelievably ingenious interlocking connectors — many of them leaked, wracked, delaminated, or experienced some sort of material fatigue. Yet jointitis — a disease increasingly prevalent among theorists in prefabrication — continued to spread. One of prefabrication's most illustrious pioneers designed a joint to connect two or more wooden panels; it was a miracle of ingenuity, and required little more from the on-site joiners than a doctorate in Chinese puzzling. The pioneer, it seemed, had never been told of an earlier and less sophisticated joint used in wood-framing, known as the nail.

The ''celebration of the joint'' — the elaborate articulation of every seam, of every single connection, in the making of a building — became almost a moral, a religious issue for most modern architects. It may have begun with the ''Russian Constructivists,'' whose projects (largely unbuilt) of the years after 1917 were manifestos of mechanization and of industrialization. To them, the image of the machine was a sort of animal made up of clearly articulated elements of steel, glass, and other ''modern'' materials, all joined visibly and expressively so that each element retained its own identity and its interaction with all other elements was left unmistakably clear. It was a charming — and charmingly naïve — image of the machine age; and it left an indelible imprint upon all architects of the International Style. Thus, in certain kinds of panelized or otherwise prefabricated buildings, the joint between parts — that endlessly troublesome and endlessly multiplied joint, the source of leaks, of buckling, of corrosion, of discoloration, of much fuss and bother and expense — this miserable joint was not merely *not* covered up and done away with as best as possible; it was intricately articulated, interminably expressed, volubly discussed by the critics, and masochistically celebrated. For, to anyone even remotely familiar with the facts of building, that damnable joint was, quite simply, modern architecture's Achilles' heel.

41

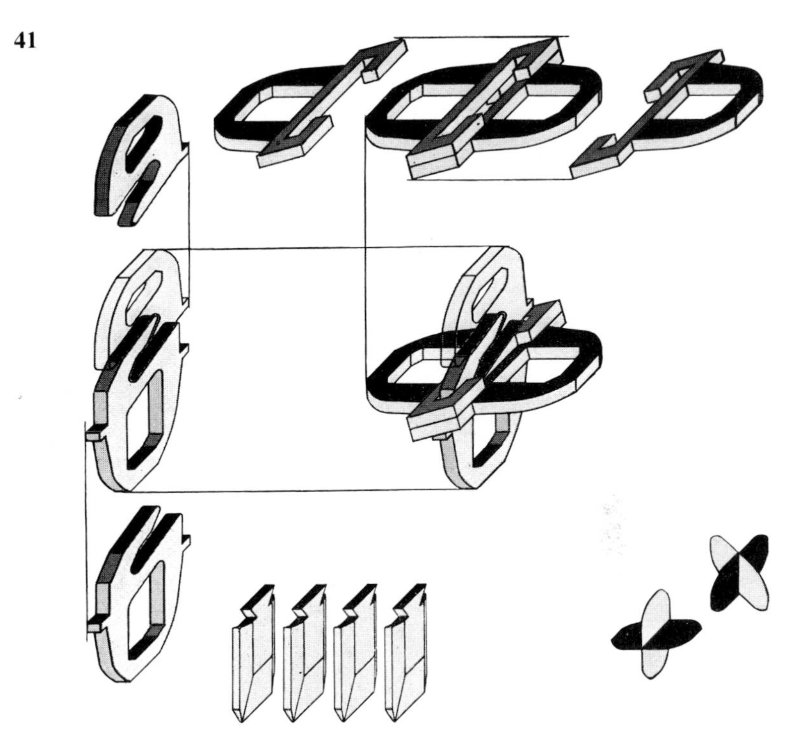

42

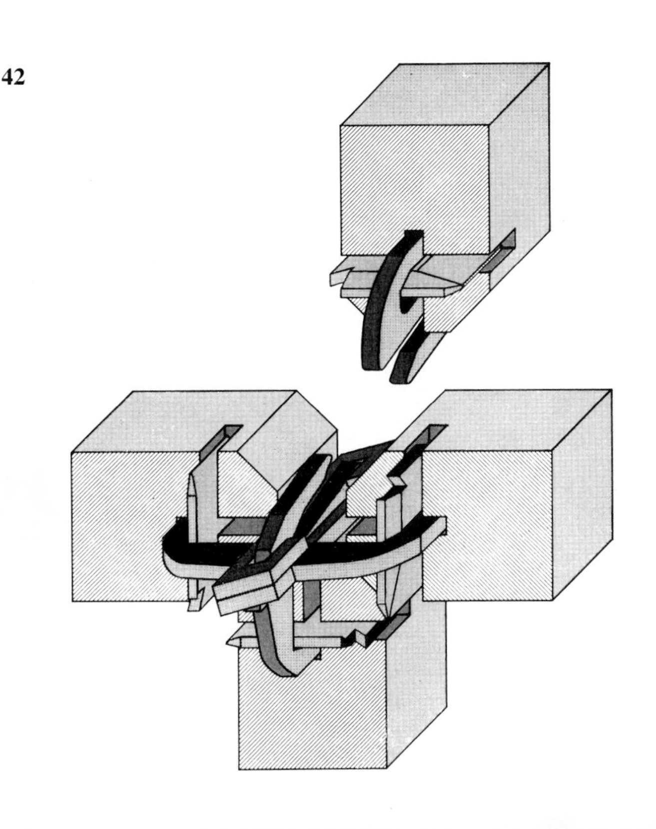

43 Prefabricated hotel-room module being hoisted into position at the A-framed Contemporary Hotel in Walt Disney World, Florida.

43

Almost every single system of prefabrication advanced in the United States during the 1930s, 1940s, and 1950s (and most of those advanced to the present day) was a panel system, designed in theory to simplify, speed up, and reduce the cost of the building shell. Every one of these systems seemed to employ its own kind of joint — a neoprene gasket, an ingenious interlock, or some adhesive butt. Many of these systems also subscribed to some special, carefully rationalized modular dimension — though most of them, admittedly, bowed to a four-inch module, which, amusingly enough, happens to be the module of one of the few truly prefabricated items in U.S. building today (and for centuries before): the brick.

Alas, very, very few of these systems recognized one essential fact about American building in the twentieth century: that the shell of any building may, very possibly, be the very *least* expensive single item in the total cost of construction. So that the prefabrication of the shell — which may account for no more than 20 percent of the total cost of many a building, and often accounts for less (and which may be reduced by a mere quarter, at best, through prefabrication) — will, under the very best of circumstances, save you less than a tiny fraction of one year's interest due on the building's mortgage! In short, the whole endlessly meticulous, beautifully reasoned, and exquisitely detailed systems of panelized construction may not justify themselves in any terms other than advancing their designers' progress toward their chosen heaven. Much, much more might have been accomplished to reduce the horrendous cost of building all over the world if architects had devoted themselves to help enact legislation that would outlaw untrammeled speculation with the price of land, or to help construct financing arrangements that would not soak a homeowner (or a tenant) for the benefit of a mortgage bank.

That is the real world of building, not the world of the theoretician, and every experienced architect and developer knows this to be true. Prefabrication, as advocated in the United States over the past thirty or forty years, is a delightful intellectual exercise without much relationship to the manner in which most buildings are made. American (and most other) buildings are, in fact, shaped not by their architects and builders, but by moneylenders.

Still, no one in his or her right mind rejects this basic premise: building must be industrialized, must be mass-produced, in order to keep up with the needs of people in the developed and, especially, the developing and underdeveloped nations. The argument is simply over how this is to be accomplished.

One answer may be found in a seemingly insignificant event reported in the *New York Times* late in 1973: a medium-sized factory had just been constructed in upstate New York. It was built in record time and at a cost significantly below the agreed budget. The weather there is bad for six months out of twelve, and terrible for the rest of the year; and so the nameless genius who constructed that modest factory had rented a large plastic bubble, inflated it to cover the entire site, and constructed his building inside this temporary man-made environment, unhampered by rain, snow, sleet, or frost. (It is easy to heat the air that holds up pneumatic structures — or to cool it — so one can literally create his own climate within.)

The factory in question was very ordinary in terms of construction — concrete block, brick, some steel trusses, and some stock windows. It was not especially modular, and not especially advanced in technological terms — and certainly not in aesthetic terms. But it was a highly advanced building in terms of construction management. Not an hour's time was lost to bad weather; no building components, piled up on the bubble-covered site, were lost to rot or rust or vandalism. No paint was applied to damp surfaces; no concrete was poured in inclement weather, and thus exposed to the danger of ultimate cracking or worse. What that nameless genius had done, knowingly or not, was to move the factory to the site — indeed, to convert his site into a building factory.

The upstate New York genius was not the first American builder to have come up with this idea. In 1926 a man called H. M. Stucker, in Lawrence, Kansas, constructed his family's "English" villa under a temporary 125-foot-by-70-foot circus tent, and he managed to get it built in record time and well below the then current building costs. The villa is still a local landmark. The same sorts of techniques have been used in Siberia and northern Canada, where buildings are routinely — and conventionally — constructed under temporary shelters to resist the fierce elements.

A rather different process was followed, in the early 1970s, at Walt Disney World, near Orlando, Florida. There, in that most adventurous of all recent "new towns" in America, the U.S. Steel Corporation, seduced by the pronunciamentos of the Modern Movement, erected a highly sophisticated prefabrication plant.

This plant turned out some fifteen hundred hotel-room modules in record time — steel-framed, flawlessly finished inside and out, completely wired, plumbed, and equipped with heating and air-conditioning ducts. The sleek modules measured about 15 feet wide, 9 feet tall, and 40 feet long. They were manufactured under optimum controlled conditions within that U.S. Steel factory, after which they were lifted onto flatbed trucks and wheeled to the sites of two large hotels on the edge of a lovely artificial lake in the center of Walt Disney World. No prefabrication effort had ever produced a better-engineered module; by comparison, Montreal's Habitat seemed almost like the work of a caveman. The lighting within the hotel-room modules even included fixtures, on dimmers that could exude artificial (but quite romantic) moonlight; and much of the furniture (as well as all bathroom fixtures) had been built-in at the prefabbing plant.

Two hotels were eventually built, using these miraculous giant "building blocks"; then the plant was dismantled and a third hotel was constructed, using entirely conventional building materials and methods.

The reason for this regressive move was simple: the conventionally built hotel turned out to cost about 30 percent less per square foot than its unconventionally built, progressively engineered predecessors. Yet it was impossible for any layman to tell the difference between the two sets of hotel-room units; if anything, the conventionally built hotel seemed more spacious in its accommodations. Admittedly, it did not offer artificial moonlight on dimmers.

What had happened was this. The exquisitely prefabricated hotel-room modules turned out in that U.S. Steel factory were trucked to the building site, where they sat and waited until the building's structural and mechanical framework was ready to accept them. While sitting and waiting, the modules were exposed to weather (which wrecked some of the beautiful finishes, and twisted some of the neat dimensional tolerances) and to vandalism (which did the rest). So when the time finally came to hoist these modules into their respective building frames, so much remedial work had to be done on the site that the initial savings were rapidly wiped out.

These two examples — the bubble that worked, and the one that burst — suggest that problems in the real world of building are rather different from those envisaged and theoretically solved in most of the think tanks of modern architecture.

What seems to be needed, in order to provide our world with the housing and other building stock it desperately needs, is a highly pragmatic understanding of how things really get constructed in this century. Obviously, industrialized building is part and parcel of our lives. But the intelligent management of building components, building labor, and building finances may do a great deal more to fill our increasingly desperate building needs than the development of still another panel system with still another kind of universal joint.

In the real world of building some other, fascinating innovations have taken place that have generally escaped the notice of theoreticians. Not only have practical builders constructed impressive buildings under temporary, man-made umbrellas, but practical engineers have created structures the size of the Seagram Building, *off the site*, and then wheeled them into position and plugged them into their infrastructures of services. Where? Well, for example, at Cape Kennedy, where huge gantries, the size of forty-story skyscrapers — complete with elevators, stairs, plug-in (and prefabbed) workshops, utility lines, and much, much more — are regularly assembled off-site and then rolled into position, at a speed of four miles per hour, and plugged into prepared utilities and services and made ready for action. Is it inconceivable that our skyscrapers (if we must have them at all) might be similarly prefabricated and moved, in one piece, into place — instead of disrupting whole sections of our cities, day and night, during their two- or three-year construction cycle? Is it *totally* inconceivable? Surely not, if tests indicate that such off-site assemblage can be accomplished in cities, just as it has been accomplished on sand spits and on the waters.

44 "Prefabricated" — but, in fact, handmade — modular capsules at Expo '70, in Osaka, Japan.

For in the real world engineers have also built entire cities — complete with factories, housing, power plants, offices, streets, and even heliports — all prefabricated onshore in Louisiana and elsewhere and then floated or helicoptered out, in large sections, to sites in the Gulf of Mexico, to form waterborne mining towns ten or more miles offshore. No elaborate theories of prefabrication or urban design were considered; these remarkable "new towns" were designed and built *ad hoc* by people who had gained most of their experience not through theorizing, but through building.

And that, unhappily, is the crux of the matter. Most schools of architecture the world over are staffed by men and women who teach the art and science of building — without ever having built anything much at all. And in most schools of architecture students are graduated without ever having been shown how to lay a course of bricks, or how to frame so much as a doghouse.

That, surely, is one reason for the present alienation between those who design and those who build. Very few of the certified masters of modern architecture received their training at the academies. Mies van der Rohe started as a mason; Le Corbusier's incisive vision was shaped by the discipline of traditional watchmaking in his hometown in Switzerland. Marcel Breuer taught himself in a carpentry shop at the Bauhaus in, first, Weimar and, later, in Dessau; then he moved on to other crafts, like pipe-bending and stonemasonry, before he concerned himself with what he called "that one percent, which is Art"; and Frank Lloyd Wright taught himself the ways in which nature constructed its miraculous organisms, and emerged from those studies as a great architect capable of great building.

Some of these masters were ultimately persuaded to turn from the realities of building to the mythology of modern technology. But, because they knew what the real world of building was all about, they kept their options open. Mies, despite earlier lip service to miracle materials, continued to build with bricks; Le Corbusier, who lived to see his hard-edged houses of the 1920s crumble, turned to brute, handmade concrete, and brick; Breuer came to similar conclusions, and began to use stone; and Frank Lloyd Wright never really fell into the technological trap in the first place.

But most teachers of architecture now, at schools of architecture around the globe, never really learned how to build. Their lessons are paper lessons, their theories, paper theories. And paper does not stand up terrifically well in the outside world.

And most prefabricators of buildings, in the United States and elsewhere, seem to be hoisted on their own preconceptions, or on the preconceptions to which the Modern Movement has subscribed from its beginnings: that industrialization and prefabrication are, in fact, the wave of the future.

It is really quite possible that the exact opposite is true.

In April 1975, the population of the globe reached the four billion mark, having just about doubled in the previous forty-five years. This terrifying statistic means, among many other things, that the building industry and others are about to become increasingly labor-intensive. In other words, it means that handcrafted buildings may very possibly solve the planet's problems much more effectively than assembly-line buildings. It seems quite likely that the wave of the future, in building and in other fields of endeavor, will be to turn away from expensive and problematical systems of prefabrication, and to entrust the job to those billions of available and desperately willing hands laying even greater billions of bricks and blocks, or framing billions of feet of joists and studs — especially in the underdeveloped and developing countries, but in developed nations as well.

Not long ago, the Indian architect B. V. Doshi, who had been schooled by such modern masters as Le Corbusier and Louis Kahn, said that the only promising way of meeting the terrible housing and other needs of his country was to go back to building with sticks and with bricks made of mud and straw. For one thing, he pointed out, those materials cost no petrodollars; for another, India (and the rest of the world) had no shortage of available and willing hands. He was probably right; in any event, the dazzling promise of modern building technology — gleaming metals, plastics, and adhesives — has failed India much as it has failed other parts of the world. (In Bangladesh, where the problems are similar, schools are now being built by CARE at half the current square-foot cost. And the secret is that the CARE experts are using a plastic reinforced not with modern fibers of glass, but with ancient vegetable fibers of jute, a material in abundant supply. The rate of construction, early in 1976, was one 20-foot-by-80-foot schoolhouse per week, which probably compares favorably with the rate of construction of schools in some developed nations.)

If Doshi and if the people at CARE are indeed right, then a severe blow has been struck at some of the basic theories that have propped up the Modern Movement from its inception. Gone, suddenly, is the cult of industrialization — with its attendant dreams of precision building and of standardization; gone, too, is Walter Gropius's amusing notion of throwaway, "Kleenex" architecture — the idea that buildings might become as disposable (or as mobile) as cars; and gone, too, is Le Corbusier's dream of a Vertical, Radiant City — because such a city cannot be built with bricks and sticks and with billions of semiskilled hands. Not even in China.

The Modern Movement has this one essential article of faith: the belief that modern technology, and all its dazzling images, would, without question, transform the world of building and the world of architecture. Everything that the modern masters proposed was, in some way, rooted in that faith. Even the formal images — the "machine look" buildings by Le Corbusier, Gropius, and Mies van der Rohe — were expressions of that faith: their razor-edged panels, their pure cubes, their shining slabs of glass, all proclaimed the advent of a glorious new world of industrialization, a world in which the immensely rational machine would replace the absurdly unpredictable sleight of hand.

And if that article of faith crumbles, and if that root of the Modern Movement is cut off, then all else may also fail.

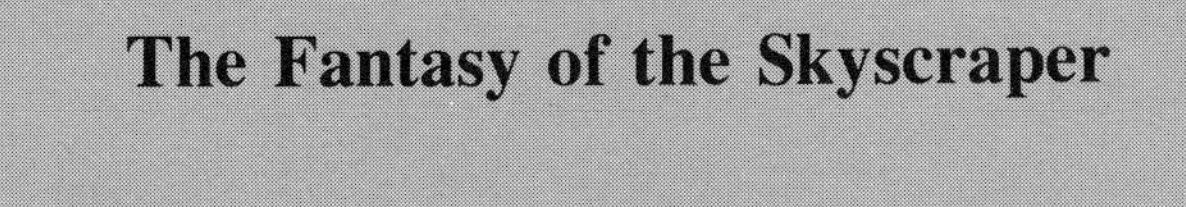

The Fantasy of the Skyscraper

The skyscraper is, quite obviously, the most visible symbol of the Modern Movement. Without it — and without the technological innovations that have made it possible — most of the new concepts in urban design developed in the first decades of the century would bite the dust. Le Corbusier's vision of the Radiant City — a community of tall buildings spaced far apart in a parklike setting — depended upon skyscraper technology to make it feasible; and all the subsequent dreams of modern architects and city planners depended, at least to some extent, upon this basic decision: to satisfy the space requirements of a rapidly expanding population, one must go up, into the clouds.

45 Skyscraper images, Sixth Avenue, Manhattan. A procession of blind façades.

46 Skyscrapers rising in the desert, near Teheran.

It is impossible to divorce the idea of the vertical city from issues of building technology (swift elevators and strong columns and beams), from issues of transportation technology (horizontal mass transit below ground level, at ground level, or slightly above it), from the issue of uncontrolled population growth, from issues of land speculation, and from issues of human interaction (do people communicate as well when assembled in vertical tubes as they do when linked by horizontal sidewalks?).

So the skyscraper, that most visible of all modern symbols, involves us in many diverse but interconnected issues. For example, it is quite possible that Le Corbusier's Radiant City is an eminently reasonable — and beautiful — alternative to urban sprawl; but it is also possible that certain critical problems in what is known as "curtain wall" technology make Le Corbusier's vision very questionable for reasons having to do with such mundane problems as high-altitude wind loads and underground water tables.

Let me try to explain. At present, the only way to construct a building fifty or a hundred stories high (within very broad budgetary constraints) is to frame it on a skeleton of steel or of reinforced concrete, and to apply a skin of relatively lightweight metal, glass, or plastic to that skeleton. If one were to build a fifty- or a hundred-story skyscraper of masonry, the walls would have to be at least a couple of dozen feet thick at ground level, which would make our land speculators (who consider the sidewalks of New York, Chicago, London, Tokyo, and Paris to be among their favorite poaching grounds) decidedly unhappy.

So the only way to construct a vertical city, as the modern masters recognized quite clearly, is to frame its buildings the way an erector set is put together: vertical columns and horizontal beams, with much space in between, and with no wasted floor area at the level of the sidewalk — or at any other level, for that matter. Which, in turn, means that the "walls" must be as thin as possible: skins or curtains of whatever lightweight material seems most suitable in the eyes of the building's designer.

47 Le Corbusier's Plan Voisin for the center of Paris, proposed in 1925.

48 More skyscrapers in the desert, near Teheran. Images of modernity die slowly.

47

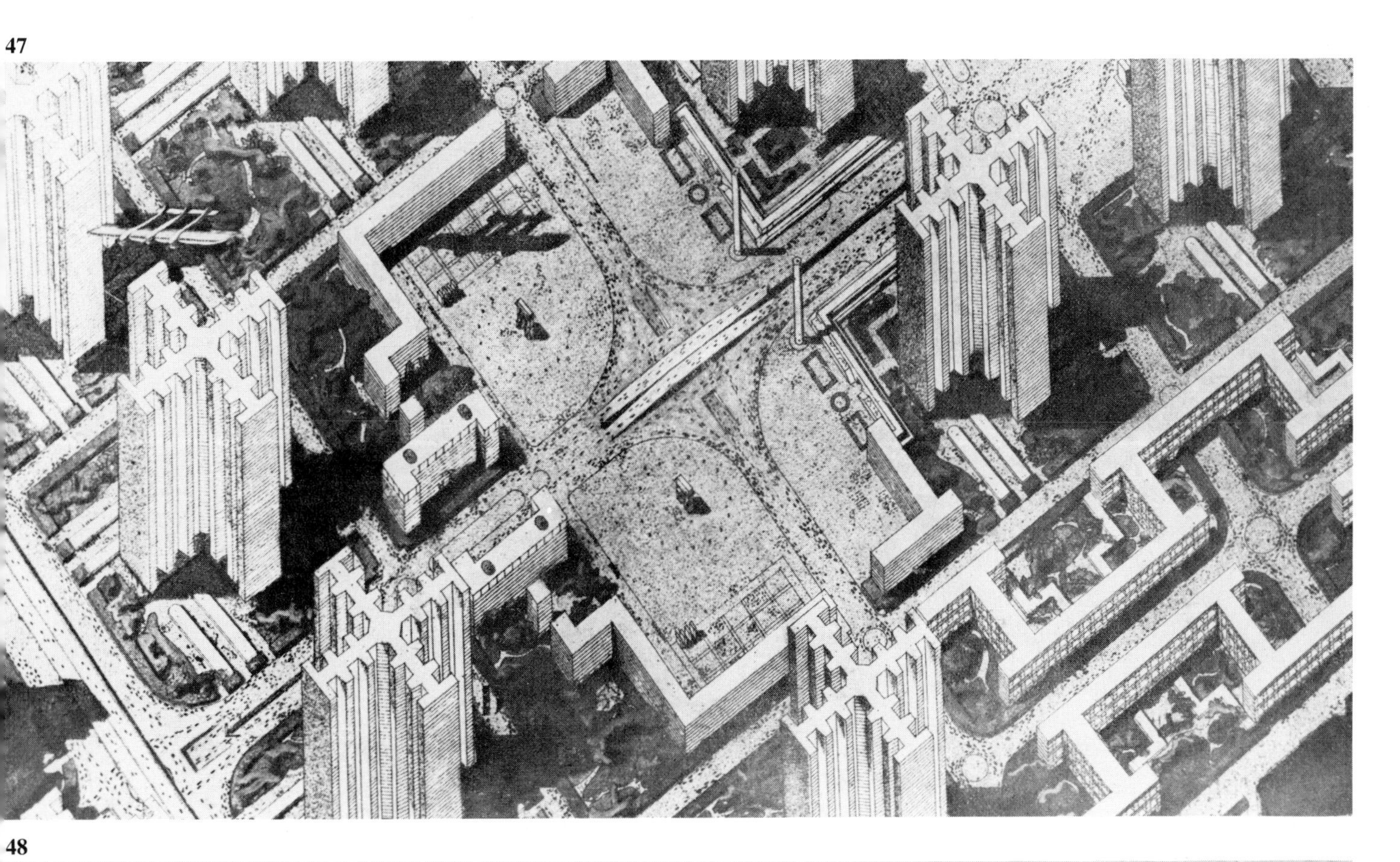

48

49, 50 Blind curtain wall images in New York and in Los Angeles, respectively. The mirrored buildings dissolve into well-deserved anonymity.

The most suitable material, in the eyes of most modern architects, has always been glass. The reasons can be found in the "purist" orientation of the Modern Movement. To the purists, the load-bearing elements of buildings — the columns and beams — should be strong and vigorously "expressed"; but the nonbearing skin or curtain wall should be just as clearly "expressed" for what it is, i.e., a mere film, an ephemeral screen, separating the indoors from the outdoors, but quite obviously without any structural capacity whatsoever.

Glass fulfilled that intention to perfection. (Nothing could be more invisible except a curtain of air, a device used occasionally for doorways into department stores and other public spaces anxious to attract multitudes.) Glass — at least in its unadulterated state, before being subjected to tinting, mirror-coating, and other surface treatments — was, quite clearly, the ideal "skin" if the purpose was to produce maximum invisibility for the wall and maximum visibility for the structural skeleton of the building.

But if the purpose was also to create a tolerable interior environment, then glass left a great deal to be desired. The heat loss (and heat gain) through a wall of one-quarter- or one-half-inch plate glass is absolutely staggering — well in excess of ten times that of a typical masonry cavity wall filled with an insulation board. The flooding of interior spaces behind glass walls with natural light benefits no one but the manufacturers of venetian blinds. And there are problems of interior condensation as well as strange updrafts outside the glass walls that have often defied solution. In 1952, for example, all five thousand windows of the UN Secretariet had to be virtually rebuilt when it was found that the pressure differential between the inside and the outside became so great in powerful rainstorms that raindrops were driven up and into the building through so-called weepholes in the double-hung windows. Those weepholes had been routinely installed to permit accumulated condensation to drain out of the building — downward, of course; but because of the curious ways in which winds and pressures affected the 540-foot-high glass wall, it rained *up* rather than *down*! This unplanned paradox has haunted the United Nations ever since.

49

50

To counteract the fundamental drawbacks in its material, the glass industry has exerted itself mightily to invent a whole series of ingenious (and expensive) products that are intended to make glass buildings fit for human habitation (and to add profits to the holders of glass company stock).

There are many tinted glasses, designed to reduce the blinding effect of living in a glass tower facing the sun; there are tinted glass-sandwiches — double-glazed panels — designed both to reduce that blinding effect and roughly to double the insulating value of the wall. There are reflective glasses, coated with silver or gold mirror-films, that may reduce glare as well as heat gain (and thus air-conditioning loads) within; and there are innumerable exterior shading devices that may or may not keep the sun's rays from ever touching the glass skin behind all this elaborate scaffolding.

Some of these ingenious inventions and devices border on the ludicrous. For example, the mirror-coated glasses successfully defeat the very objective that attracted the modern pioneers to the glass-skinned building in the first place: because the mirrored glass is utterly opaque in daytime when seen from the outside, it thus effectively conceals the very structural skeleton that the glass-skinned building was supposed to reveal so dramatically! Besides, mirror-faced buildings — all the rage from Nashville to Dallas to Teheran and beyond — have proved to be somewhat disconcerting to their neighbors. While one can, admittedly, shave in one's neighbor's wall (as I once did while standing on the balcony of an Atlanta hotel room), one cannot conveniently avoid one's neighbor's reflected heat. In Houston, an old downtown hotel successfully sued its new, mirror-faced neighbor because the latter's shiny garb dramatically increased the air-conditioning requirements of the former's guests. Meanwhile a third party — an entirely new developer of an adjacent parcel of land — announced that he was about to erect still another mirror-faced building, this one presumably angled to incinerate the original offender's tenants.

The prospect of a city made up entirely of mirrored façades, blindly reflecting back and forth into each other and into infinity, is not without its charm, especially if you happen to be the fairest one of all — i.e., the one and only building in a neighborhood that boasts a real façade, and can therefore see itself reflected ad infinitum in all directions. Certain southern and southwestern U.S. cities are rapidly attaining this distinction, as indeed they should, since none of them contains more than one or two buildings worth looking at in any case.

But the prospect of a giant Hall of Mirrors, or Skyline of Mirrors, should chill the blood of anyone who does, in fact, care about the looks of buildings — e.g., an architect. It implies, of course, total abdication. The great Ludwig Mies van der Rohe, the coolest of all the masters of the Modern Movement, sketched an all-glass skyscraper as early as 1919. He built it (and three others) on Lake Shore Drive, in Chicago, some thirty years later, and in one of the four towers he reserved an apartment for himself. "The important thing in a glass tower," Mies had said in 1919, "is the play of reflections." Being an enormously rational man, he realized that "the play of reflections" is best observed not from inside the glass tower, *but from across the street* — which is precisely where his old apartment happened to be located. So he never moved into that apartment set aside for him in his own glass tower; he preferred to contemplate the reflections from his old brick and stone apartment house half a block away.

Mies never would have tolerated the attachment of elaborate exterior blind mechanisms to any of his buildings. Such mechanisms not only conceal whatever goes on behind all that gadgetry (and thus mask not only the skeleton but the skin as well), but they also create one or two further problems — how to clean the exterior gadgetry, how to clean the glass behind it, and, finally, how to keep ice from forming on the exterior blinds in northern climates during the winter months, in order to save innocent passersby from the terminal effects of falling icicles. (Answer: built-in electric heating systems, to melt the ice on the blinds that are supposed to shade the glass that would admit too much summer heat if it were not shaded — which blinds might thus save the owners of the glass-skinned building some of the cost of their interior consumption of electricity used to air-condition their glass-walled buildings!)

51 Saul Steinberg's clairvoyant drawing, done 25 years before the Hancock Tower was built. (Copyright 1951, Saul Steinberg.)

51

Copyright 1950 Cowles Magazines, Inc., reprinted by permission of Flair.

This situation may well be sufficiently grotesque in itself. It becomes even more so when one examines certain technical aspects of those brilliantly innovative glass skins that sheathe office cubage from pole to equator and to that other pole.

The double-glazed insulating sandwiches (with or without mirror-coating, with or without tinting) are clearly in need of some urgent remedial research. Nobody, as of this writing, knows for sure what caused some of the ten thousand mirror-coating and double-glazed windows to fall out of Boston's stunningly elegant John Hancock Tower — or what caused the rest of them to threaten to follow suit. And nobody may ever know. But now that these ten thousand mirror-coated and double-glazed "lights" have been replaced, it seems possible, in the minds of some experts, that there might have been certain original failings in the material itself that would hardly be tolerated by the aircraft industry, say, or by any other industry concerned with the safety of passengers and bystanders, as the building industry should be.

For example, it turns out that there may occur a certain ultraviolet buildup inside those double-glazed wall sandwiches that can (and often does) play havoc with the strip of sealants that completes the sides and top edges of these sandwiches. This buildup could cause the sealants to "pump out," leaving the sheets of glass relatively free to move out of their metal frames and, ultimately, to pop — and then to slice the craniums of any heedless pedestrians. There may (or may not) be a way of solving this particular problem before half of our urban population has been wiped off the map, but it is clearly a matter of some concern that the building industry continues to market products whose performance it does not understand, products, moreover, that dramatically undercut the very foundations of the architecture the industry pretends to serve.

It may seem that I am picking nits; but it is not inconceivable that certain implacable facts of life — or of building technology — will place in doubt many, if not most, of the fundamental tenets of the Modern Movement.

52 Boston's John Hancock Tower, after it had shed most of its mirrored curtain wall. The dark surfaces are painted plywood.

52

For instance, not only does the tall, glass-skinned building present problems of a magnitude not even remotely recognized to this day, but the tall, curtain-walled building — glass-skinned or not — presents problems even further removed from current recognition, such as problems of structural analysis and resolution.

Few people outside the professions of architecture and engineering know that the structural design of a skyscraper is not primarily determined by the loads transmitted by its many heavy floors to the ground on which the building stands, *but by the wind loads that a skyscraper must resist in order to keep its balance.* For a tall building acts very much like a huge sail, and it can easily be blown over unless its "keel" — that is, its foundation — is deep and strong. In fact, the shape of the foundation of a tall building is determined not so much by its height as by the acres of exterior wall surface that face the winds.

53

In a skin-and-bones building, in which the exterior walls are made of a film of glass (or of a similarly fragile material), it becomes necessary to build massive, expensive, diagonal cross-bracing into the skyscraper — for the principal reason that the exterior skin is not rigid enough, or cannot be attached to the columns and beams rigidly enough, to help resist the horizontal pressures that build up during high winds. In other words, the ideal skin-and-bones building could, conceivably, be twisted out of whack unless it were cross-braced between columns and beams much in the way that a radio or TV tower is cross-braced. If the "skin" were more substantial, and made of a material that could be more firmly attached to the bones behind it without impairing the aesthetic sensibilities of its designer, there would be much less need for massive and expensive interior cross-bracing — and less need for massive and expensive foundations.

Every New York taxi driver has known for years that the Empire State Building, though largely faced with stone, sways in a storm (or even in a breeze), and that a trip to its top on windy days is likely to induce nausea. But not until very recently have tall or even low building been subjected to reliable wind-tunnel tests. The results (recorded on film, while smoke was introduced into the wind tunnels) have been startling: at various altitudes, and under various wind conditions, tall buildings and their walls (or skins) are buffeted in a way that would alarm any experienced sailor.

53, 54, 55 Large windswept plazas ringed by skyscrapers may make for striking compositions, but they do not guarantee pedestrian bliss — especially on breezy days.

Tall buildings and their smooth walls are not the only victims of buffeting. Pedestrians who walk past tall, smooth-skinned skyscrapers may be subjected to what someone has called the Mary Poppins syndrome: during high winds, the airstream blocked by the broad side of a tall, flat building will be deflected in two directions — some of it upward, most of it spiraling to the ground, creating a so-called standing vortex (or mini-tornado) at sidewalk level. This amusing encounter may not invariably lift the pedestrian off his or her feet, or induce pirouettes or even nausea, but it will rarely improve the quality of urban life.

55

The quality of urban life is even less improved if the tall building is set on stilts or, as Le Corbusier called them, "pilotis." It was axiomatic to many of his urban design theories that buildings should be raised off the ground in this fashion. He had pointed out repeatedly, throughout his career, that this device would free the ground floor of the city and leave it open for pedestrians to traverse it, unhampered by buildings that would normally block their paths. It was an important and imaginative notion; unhappily, it is also a diagram almost guaranteed to sweep pedestrians off their feet under certain quite common wind conditions: a downdraft from a tall building on pilotis, or any direct, horizontal wind current, will be greatly accelerated as it becomes compressed and is forced to pass through the restricted opening under a building. The resulting "venturi effect" — a well-known phenomenon in aerodynamics (especially as it relates to buildings and spaces between or under them) — is one of those physical phenomena that the Modern Movement has ignored from its beginning, and continues to ignore. Complexes such as New York's World Trade Center have spacious, semienclosed pedestrian plazas at ground level; but because these plazas are almost certain to have openings between enclosing buildings — at corners, or somewhere in the middle — winds are literally sucked into them and invited to howl through them at greatly accelerated speeds, thus making the plaza a place to be strenuously avoided.

Most of these facts are only just beginning to dawn upon architects of skyscrapers — more than fifty years after the Vertical City was proclaimed as the prototype for an anxious and rapidly expanding world. One reason is that *smooth*-skinned skyscrapers, a fairly recent development, generate wind currents very different from those generated by the rough-hewn skyscrapers of the 1920s and 1930s. Another reason is that not until about 1970 have architects and structural engineers been able to use really reliable wind tunnels in which to test tall buildings and their sheer walls. And not until quite recently have architects and structural engineers been able to plot the airstreams generated in cities built on the gridiron plan and frequently interrupted by open pedestrian plazas — designed to generate civic bliss, but more often, in fact, populated by desperate stragglers buffeted by vortices, lurching toward the nearest exit. (Whenever the grand pedestrian plaza is also graced by spectacular fountains, as it frequently is, the desperate stragglers are very likely to be drenched before they clutch the door to that nearest exit, while cursing the designers of that civic bliss.)

There are other unsolved problems that make skyscraper living uncomfortable, to say the least, and occasionally detrimental to one's health. Tall buildings often act much like the flues that draw smoke out of a fireplace — and the taller they are, the more efficient they are in generating spectacular updrafts. Unless expensive (and often unfeasible) air-pressuring systems are installed within the public areas of a tall apartment building, for example, the elevator shafts will act as flues, and elevator doors will close only with great difficulty during high winds. In one such building in which I lived for several years, the hallways could not be adequately pressurized; thus, if a tenant had the temerity to open a window in the apartment, a roar comparable to that of a jet engine would develop, and winds would howl through the apartment and out into the public hallways (through the unclosable crack under one's front door), sweeping everything off tables and shelves located in their path. On one occasion, when I finally succeeded in opening my front door despite the enormous air pressure holding the door in place, a bedroom door *inside* the apartment crashed shut with such force that its steel frame was knocked clean out of the plaster wall. If a small child had happened to be standing in that doorway, it would have been killed.

The trouble with these problems is that they are virtually insoluble, in technological terms, unless some very major and unlikely innovations occur in the control of the external and internal environment. So far, none is in sight. Some astonishing remedial devices have been installed in tall buildings that sway too much in the wind: in the ill-fated, sixty-two-story John Hancock Tower, in Boston, a so-called dual-tuned mass damper system had to be installed on the fifty-eighth floor when it was discovered that the tower might sway rather disconcertingly under certain wind conditions. This "dual-tuned mass damper" consists of something like six hundred tons of lead and steel, and the mass is designed to move in opposition to the direction of strong winds. The system cost $3 million to install in the John Hancock Tower; in other skyscrapers the cost has been considerably higher.

Such grotesque remedies will not alter the facts of life on earth, and natural forces are not very likely to be abolished in the foreseeable future.

Tall buildings, as we have seen, require unusually deep foundations. The reason is that deep foundations will help them resist wind loads, and thus prevent them from toppling. All this is obvious. Less obvious is the fact that deep excavations for deep foundations and deep basements create a serious menace to many older neighbors of the new skyscraper; for when you excavate deeply you must, of course, prop up your neighbor's foundations, but this may not save them if you also have to install pumps to reduce the water pressure on your new basement walls and floor — below the surface of the existing townscape. When you install such pumps, you begin to lower the water table in your immediate neighborhood, and when you do *that*, you may seriously endanger nearby landmarks that, like the palazzi of Venice, were probably constructed on wooden piles.

Wooden piles under palazzi will last for centuries, *if submerged*, but once the water table drops, and the wooden piles are exposed to air, they will start to rot — and the buildings they were built to support may start to crumble. This is especially true in a city like Boston, which is built very largely on man-made landfill. The designers of a skeletal tower next to a Richardsonian church of the nineteenth century may believe that they are creating an exciting and vibrant change of urban scale by erecting their skin-and-bones tower next to some of the architectural heritage they truly respect; but their structural engineers know better — and they know just how unexpectedly vibrant the change may turn out to be!

So we now have this extraordinary chain of circumstance that seriously challenges one of the most unchallengeable precepts of the Modern Movement. The skyscraper, built of steel or concrete bones and draped with a skin of glass, cannot contain an interior environment that humanity can either suffer or afford; moreover, for reasons having to do with structural facts rather than modern technocratic myths, this same sort of structure cannot help but erode or extinguish the older, surrounding urban fabric. So the Modern Movement's ideal — the Radiant City — is revealed, in fact, as the inevitable ravager of our urban heritage. Not the intentional ravager necessarily — though some of the modern pioneers did, quite clearly, act with malice aforethought — but certainly the unwitting ravager of our urban heritage.

All of this is really quite disturbing if you happen to be an architect enamored with the ideals of a dream world, but functioning, willy-nilly, in the real. Your ideals are those of the modern masters, but the moment of truth occurs when the contractors' bids are in, and you find that the real world cannot afford the dream. And you might, in fact, consider it a nightmare — and not in economic terms alone. Admittedly, man or woman does not live by bread alone. But if a great work of art, designed along the precepts established by your masters, turns out to be a disaster in human terms as well, then perhaps the time has come to take stock.

There is no doubt that the Vertical City — the Radiant City of Le Corbusier and Hilberseimer and Mies van der Rohe and all the rest — is an eminently rational solution for an irrational planet (unless, of course, the proliferation of the Pill takes care of the problem to which Le Corbusier devoted much of his life). But is the Vertical City, in fact, the most desirable human habitat? Is it worth fighting for? Is it even a desirable alternative to low-rise living, or to suburban sprawl?

The answer quite clearly is no. In the Vertical City, the sidewalk is replaced by the elevator. The sidewalk, a place of conversation and confrontation, is replaced by a capsule, a mute place enlivened occasionally by piped-in jukebox melodies. In the Vertical City, the garden is replaced by a concrete window box labeled "balcony." In the Vertical City, your neighbor is your enemy, the person who hammers nails into the other side of your wall. In the Vertical City, interior ventilation ducts convey to you the breakup of a marriage in Apartment 27D and the despondency of a French poodle in 30G. In the Vertical City, these are likely to be the only human and animal contacts. In the Vertical City, alienation is complete.

Much has been written to document these assertions and to explain the reasons. It is not inconceivable that certain kinds of vertical cities could be designed to foster neighborliness and brotherly love, but the facts and figures so far adduced make this seem highly unlikely. (As pointed out later in this book, you can only cram so many human beings, per linear foot, onto a "sidewalk in the sky" on the fifth floor, say, of a "linear city," a couple of dozen stories high; but you would have no trouble at all cramming ten times that number onto *real* sidewalks along streets lined with five-story buildings.)

Much has also been written to document the perfectly obvious fact that families with young children are best served by houses with manageable gardens, where the kids can frolic safely by themselves (under remote supervision) until such time as they frolic in groups in equally safe and equally manageable communal gardens.

And a great deal has been said and written to the effect that today's American suburbia — single little houses on single little lots, strung out on boring and expensive streets ad infinitum — does not represent the only alternative to high-rise living; that, in fact, there are perfectly good rowhouse solutions, and medium-rise apartment solutions, and mixed-rise communities with even a skyscraper here and there, which can provide a better life than either the Vertical City or horizontal suburbia.

But not much has been said or written to put to rest, once and for all, the Modern Movement's infatuation with Le Corbusier's concept of *La Ville Radieuse*, a concept that dominated much modern urban design from 1922 to the day, in the 1970s, when the first of Pruitt-Igoe's semi–high-rise buildings, in St. Louis, had to be dynamited because there was just no way this depressing project, built in the 1950s, could be made humanly habitable. (Pruitt-Igoe's high-rise buildings, by the way, were also equipped with "sidewalks in the sky." They didn't work.) Pruitt-Igoe's buildings were framed in concrete and faced with a veneer of brick. If they had been substantially taller, the exterior walls would undoubtedly have had to be of a material lighter in weight than masonry, and the façades might well have been handsomer. But it wouldn't have made much difference. "Communities" of exclusively tall buildings, spaced far apart, and sealed off from the outside world both physically and philosophically, are inherently doomed, and no architectural cosmetics can save them.

56

56 "Sidewalks in the sky" (like these in London) are not a viable alternative to sidewalks on the ground — where the action usually is.

Every modern architect not obsessed with the need to document his manhood in public has known, from the beginning of his time, that the skyscraper is the death of cities. He has known (women architects are rarely as enamored of skyscrapers as men are) that skyscrapers destroy human interaction, that they cause enormous congestion at the ground-floor levels of cities, and that they tend to drive out smaller-scale — human-scale — buildings through economic pressure by raising neighboring land values and real estate taxes, and thus forcing low-rise neighbors to sell out to high-rise developers. Frank Lloyd Wright's preposterous scheme for a mile-high tower in the Chicago Loop, advanced in his declining years, was clearly a tongue-in-cheek swipe at his favorite enemy, the high-rise metropolis. He understood, one feels, that the building of his mile-high tower probably would have wiped out the rest of the city, or most of it, which may very well have been his intention. "Decenter and reintegrate" was Wright's most succinct urban axiom. The converse, "centralize and disintegrate," is the principle that shaped his tower. He must have sensed that this was so; and having spent much of his life fighting against land speculation, he must have enjoyed the prospect.

Most of the other modern pioneers were less devious in their advocacies and much more outspoken in their professed beliefs. All of them, at some point in their careers, railed against land speculation and espoused vaguely socialist causes of one sort or another. Yet, when the chips were down, most of them proved entirely willing to supply ethereal motives to prop up their avaricious clients: the land developer was looking for the fastest buck in sight, and the modern pioneer was perfectly willing to sanctify the search by advancing all sorts of idealistic notions that seemed to justify the Vertical City in the sight of God. For there is really only one justification for building such atrocities as Upper Sixth Avenue in Manhattan — and that is cash.

If you are a land speculator, fully legitimated by the free enterprise system to squeeze every last profitable dollar out of the planet earth, then you will sell your square footage to the next profiteer up the ladder for the highest attainable price; and then that profiteer will sell to the banks, or to some developer, up another rung of that same ladder; and then that bank will propose a skyscraper that will rent at a cost, per square foot, that will wipe out every neighborhood tenant, and every neighborhood store, and drive them into the suburbs or into bankruptcy, or both.

And at that point there will be an idealistic modern architect who will provide the developer with an idealistic underpinning; and at that point, too, there will be an embattled community — without funds, without hope, but with plenty of guts — and the modern architect, who helped invent the Ideal City, will be on the side of the exploiter.

That exploiter shapes the modern skyscraper more decisively than any modern architect in his employ. Skyscraper curtain walls are no longer designed by architects, but by real estate salesmen; today, the rentable square footage in an American office tower is measured from glass skin to glass skin (not from the edge of the interior, carpeted floor to the opposite edge). This means that every skyscraper developer insists upon pushing the glassline of his building out as far as the laws determining the shape of the "envelope" will permit, with no projections beyond that line. The result is a building package, tightly and smoothly wrapped in glass, that will generate as much rentable interior space as possible. Any building that boasts an irregular exterior wall, with projections and indentations that might cast interesting shadows (and disperse high-velocity up- and downdrafts), may generate as much as 8 to 10 percent less in rentable floor area than a building with a sheer, smooth skin that projects blandness and boredom to the outside world (and helps generate fierce mini-tornadoes at sidewalk level).

57

57 Housing development in Isfahan, Iran, replaced conventional sidewalks with elevated "sidewalks" on upper floors.

58 Sooner or later, skyscraper developments will destroy low-rise communities next door — by increasing land values, or taxes, or both.

58

So the Modern Movement, which grew out of a passionate involvement with the human condition, has, via the skyscraper, become the chief apologist for the real estate speculator. Wolf von Eckardt, the *Washington Post* critic who knew Constantinos Doxiades, recently quoted the late architect and city planner as having said, in a colloquium in 1971: ''My greatest crime was the construction of high-rise buildings.''

And then Doxiades enumerated the ''crimes'' to which he had confessed earlier:

''One: the most successful cities of the past were those where people and buildings were in a certain balance with nature. But high-rise buildings work against nature, or, in modern terms, against the environment. They destroy the scale of the landscape and obstruct normal air circulation, so causing automotive and industrial discharges to collect in pockets of severe pollution which cannot easily be dispersed.

''Two: high-rise buildings work against man himself, because they isolate him from others, and this isolation is an important factor in the rising crime rate. Children suffer even more because they lose their direct contacts with nature, and with other children. Even when contacts can be maintained, they are subject to parental control. Both children, and parents, suffer as a result.

''Three: high-rise buildings work against society because they prevent the units of social importance — the family . . . the neighborhood, etc. — from functioning as naturally and as normally as before.

''Four: high-rise buildings work against networks of transportation, communication, and of utilities, since they lead to higher densities, to overloaded roads, to [more extensive] water supply systems — and, more importantly, because they form vertical networks which create many additional problems — crime being just one of them.

''Five: high-rise buildings destroy the urban landscape by eliminating all values which existed in the past. Human symbols — such as churches, mosques, temples of all kinds, city halls, which once arose above the city — are now below the skyscrapers. We may not agree that God or government should rise above man, but are we ready to agree that symbols of capital gain should rise above everything else . . . ?''

Doxiades was not the most profound thinker to have emerged from the Modern Movement, but he was one of the more sensitive. And the questions he posed are not frivolous. ''In our fixation with architecture as a sculptural response to an economic equation,'' Harry Weese, the Chicago architect, has said, ''we have neglected the ground, the sky, and most of all, the user.''

The Fantasy of the Ideal City

59 The New Zagreb, Yugoslavia. A community of 100,000 designed and built in the image of Le Corbusier's Radiant City.

The city of Zagreb, in northern Yugoslavia, has a population of about 750,000. All but 100,000 live in the old city, north of the River Sava, in buildings and along streets, squares, and parks, some of which date back to the Middle Ages.

To the south of the River Sava, there is a new town — the new Zagreb — with a population of about 100,000. It is an impressive complex of concrete and glass towers, townhouses, schools, shops, and other community facilities, all spaced far apart and separated by generous parks, well planted and well paved. Around the perimeter of the new Zagreb there are wide superhighways that lead into the old city as well as to the surrounding countryside farther south. There are parking lots, bus stops, trolley-car stations, and even a brand-new airport. Although the new Zagreb may not measure up, in every detail of its plan or of its individual buildings, to the standards for a modern city established by such pioneers as Le Corbusier, this community of 100,000 is an impressive, updated version of Le Corbusier's *Ville Radieuse*, first proposed in the early 1920s and now the stereotype of New Towns and of urban renewal from Boston to Brasilia.

The only trouble with this *Ville Radieuse* to the south of the old Zagreb is that it is dead.

Every evening the people of Zagreb gather in the streets of the old center of town, around what is now known as the Square of the Republic. The center of the old town is jammed with pedestrians, its sidewalks crowded with cafés, its streets closed to automobiles and opened wide to young and old alike, who stroll about, chatting, window-shopping, showing off, and having the time of their lives doing it. Meanwhile, to the south of the River Sava, those great expanses of greenery between the concrete and glass apartments are deserted. No one ventures out — not for fear of crime (Yugoslavia is a civilized country), but for fear of boredom. People stay inside their modern apartments — unless, of course, they have taken off in the general direction of the old town center, to join their fellow citizens.

60 New Zagreb — impeccably built, and devoid of life.

61, 62 The old Zagreb. The Square of the Republic is a daily and nightly gathering place for young and old alike — and especially for those who live in the Radiant City across the river.

60

The new Zagreb, a *Ville Radieuse* almost par excellence, is a dead city, a place of loneliness and alienation; whereas the old Zagreb, designed by no one, and made seemingly unworkable by the invasion of the automobile — this is where the action is. And here, in these old and not very convenient houses, live most of the architects responsible for the design of the new city!

Zagreb is merely one of hundreds of similar examples around the world. In Paris, London, Berlin (East and West), Milan, New York, Los Angeles, Osaka, and God only knows where else, there are gleaming new neighborhoods, faultlessly (or almost faultlessly) designed and planned according to the highest standards laid down by the Modern Movement — new neighborhoods as dead, much of the day and night, as the new Zagreb. And in some of these same cities there are crooked old streets bursting at the seams with people and life and commerce and entertainment, and dingy old buildings crammed full with the apartments of the very same architects who designed those sanitary, air-conditioned diagrams on the other side of the river or the tracks. (Ironically, the English-language equivalent of the official German word for "urban renewal" is "urban sanitizing." No city on earth has been more devastatingly and rigidly "sanitized" than East Berlin.)

1

62

The reasons for this failure of modern urban design are many, but I suspect that the principal reason is very simple. The ideal modern prototype — the *Villes Radieuses* of Le Corbusier, or the *Siedlungen* of the Weimar Republic — were well-intentioned diagrams scaled to the rather terrifying impending mechanization and automation of twentieth-century urban life. They were diagrams scaled to the automobile age, rather than organisms scaled to the needs of man. Le Corbusier's idealism — and the idealism of many of the other modern pioneers — was indeed touching: he proposed gleaming towers scattered among groves of trees, lawns, lakes, and streams in almost lyrical terms, speaking of man's yearning for greenery, sunlight, fresh air, and space. All very true; but man's primary yearning, it seems, is not for great expanses of open space, *but for other men* (and women and children). What these Ideal Cities of the Modern Movement lacked so dismally were small, crowded, dense spaces in which people could rub shoulders and interact — have fun, have arguments, even, if necessary, have fights. The most devastating, albeit unconscious, commentaries on those spacious Ideal Cities are the sculptor Giacometti's emaciated giants, blindly traversing vast landscapes peopled only with other similar figures passing by, mute, in a kind of procession of alienation.

What is missing from these well-intentioned diagrams for Ideal Cities is something so obvious that it has escaped the eyes of most critical observers. What is missing is *the street*, that most vibrant, exciting, irritating, and yet most stimulating of all outdoor spaces. It was replaced by parks (okay for Sundays), by squares (okay for demonstrations and public addresses), by playgrounds (child ghettos), and by shopping centers (okay for supermarket owners; not quite so okay for their customers).

But the street was gone. We were given vistas, plazas, and traumas. Some innovators in the Modern Movement — those who proposed to replace cities with "megastructures" — also proposed streets or sidewalks up in the sky, by which they meant pedestrian walkways on upper levels of contiguous ribbons of high-rise buildings, where children would frolic and their parents would stop and chat. It was a charming idea, but its logistics were flawed: "streets in the sky," or "sidewalks in the sky," are very difficult to populate with any level of density, since not very many people live on the twenty-first floor, say, of a megastructure; and "streets in the sky," or "sidewalks in the sky," are very difficult to make very interesting unless they are lined with shops, which would

63 Le Corbusier's 1925 vision of a modern, urban street.

64 Walt Disney's vision of an urban street, roughly fifty years later, built near Orlando, Florida.

63

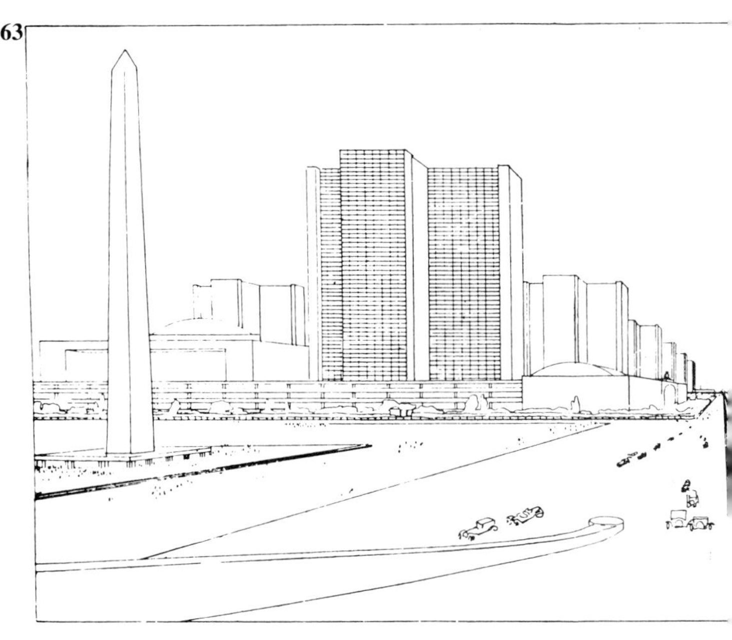

64

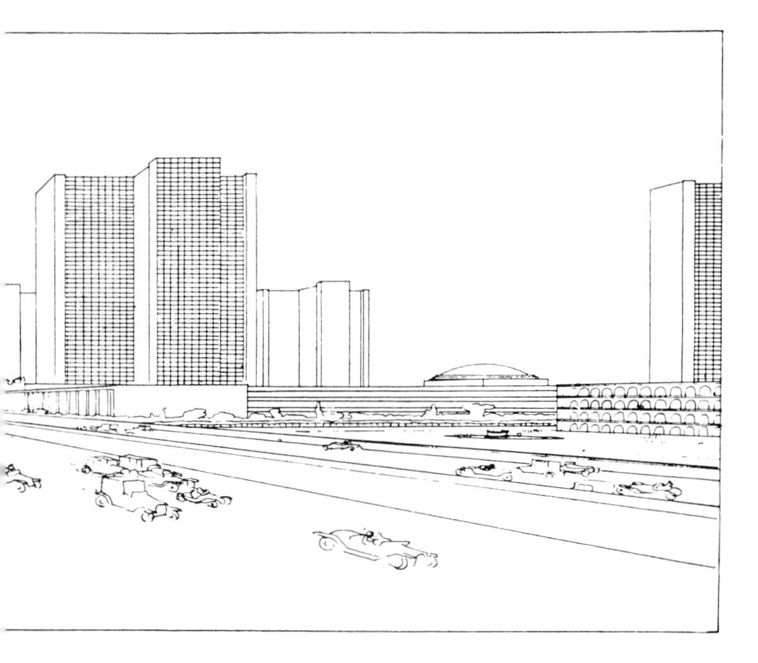

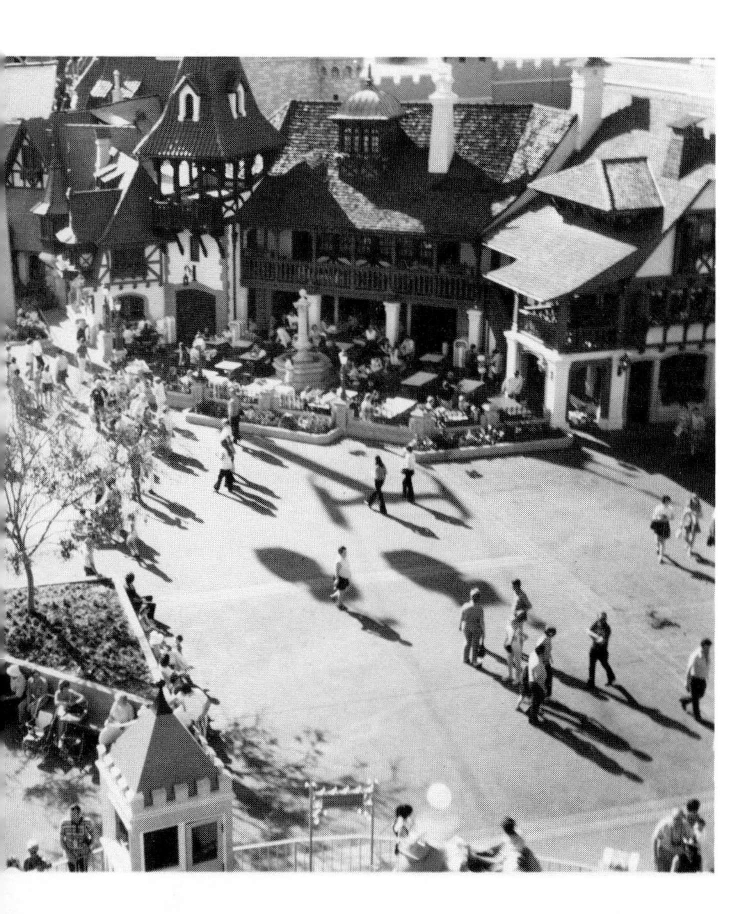

further reduce the number of people living on that hypothetical twenty-first floor. Many megastructures (or ministructures) endowed with such airborne "streets" have been built, and every one of their airborne "streets" has turned out to be a desolate concrete runway leading nowhere. A good example is Robin Hood Gardens, the high-rise apartment complex in London's East End designed by Alison and Peter Smithson and completed in 1973. Robin Hood Gardens is interesting in many ways, as are its architects; but the "sidewalks in the sky" that form the lateral circulation in these apartment blocks are excruciatingly dull and usually devoid of people. An earlier example is the double shopping "street" halfway up Le Corbusier's mammoth Unité d'Habitation in Marseilles, which had to be converted into a street of offices rather than shops, since shops do not function terrifically well without customers.

In the early 1970s, some fifty years after Le Corbusier's first sketch for a *Ville Radieuse*, the most interesting New Town built in the United States in this century was completed in a swamp some thirty miles south of Orlando, Florida. The town is known to men, women, and children everywhere as Walt Disney World, or WDW. Although WDW owns 28,000 acres of land and water, the town itself, the so-called Magic Kingdom, measures only about seventy acres in size — about four times the size of Rockefeller Center in New York. The Magic Kingdom is America's most interesting New Town because it is a town of streets. It is also, incidentally and very importantly, an urban organism, with an infrastructure of service tunnels and ducts and a superstructure of monorails and other airborne transportation systems. But above all, WDW's Magic Kingdom is a streetscape. It is jammed with people and lined with stores and restaurants and theaters. It is not, of course, a *real* town; nobody lives there, and the cute façades are gingerbread rendered in plastic.

But WDW's Magic Kingdom is, in fact, infinitely more "real" than, let us say, the new Zagreb. People jam its streets after having paid a pretty penny to do so, whereas no one in his or her right mind would pay a cent to visit those *Villes Radieuses* that the Modern Movement has built, ad nauseam, from Osaka to Washington. Some of us live in those sanitized *Villes Radieuses* because the price is right and because the plumbing frequently works. And whenever we get a chance, we visit those wonderful old towns and cities that were built to the scale of man — those wonderful old towns and cities that are crisscrossed by dark and smelly and crooked little streets of the sort that Le Corbusier sometimes referred to as "human sewers." None of us would ever think of visiting, let us say, Co-op City, The Bronx, New York. Nor does it seem very likely that our children, or generations after them, will ever be tempted to.

Not many cities outside Florida have been built primarily as tourist attractions; but beautiful and livable cities do attract people whose talents are considered valuable by commerce, industry, government, and other fairly cold-blooded employers — and ugly cities repel such people. Certain businesses — especially those dependent for their survival upon highly sophisticated research — would have to offer combat pay to attract the best specialists to such beauty spots as Omaha, Nebraska, but they have no trouble at all attracting them to Cambridge, Massachusetts, or to Berkeley — where, in fact, such people tend to congregate anyway. When Brazil, in a fit of admirable madness, decided to move its capital from the Atlantic coast several hundred miles inland to the new Brasilia, top administrators and foreign embassy personnel had to be offered what amounted to bribes to make the move to the new Ideal City. And there are innumerable other examples, in almost every country on earth that boasts an older urban civilization, to prove that the best minds and the hands with the best skills are rarely attracted to the Ideal Cities of our time.

But all of us are irresistibly attracted to old cities — real or plastic — especially if they have been recaptured from the automobile. Walt Disney World never did permit the monsters within its walls; all services, including mini supply trains, etc., are housed within a huge "infrastructure," a kind of seventy-acre basement that serves the pedestrian dreamland above, allowing performers and their accoutrements to surface at appropriate locations upstairs, and to drop out of sight on cue. The only vehicles permitted upstairs, on WDW's narrow streets, are props: steam engines and trolley cars and such. All trucks and cars are kept out of sight — and out of smell.

65

65, 66 A street on Boston's Beacon Hill, and a "street" in Boston's Charles River Park, a Radiant City that replaced a community not unlike neighboring Beacon Hill. Densities are roughly the same, but life is not.

66

67, 68, 69, 70 New Radiant City on the edge of Munich; and views of the newly "pedestrianized" Old City. One has streets, the other does not.

In the real world — in cities like Munich, for example — much the same sort of thing has been done to liberate an ancient downtown from the tyranny of the automobile. Most of Munich's *Altstadt*, or "old city," is now a pedestrian enclave, from the semicircular Stachus Square in the east to the old city hall in the west. Initially, this pedestrian mall measured more than half a mile in length and encompassed the beautiful fifteenth-century Frauenkirche and other spectacular landmarks located along narrow, medieval side streets to the north and south.

This major axis of Munich's old city was restored to pedestrians in time for the 1972 Olympics, when the city had promised to spruce itself up to welcome its many visitors. What made the Munich mall so enormously significant, however, was not only the manner in which it reapportioned urban priorities; while the mall was being cleared of cars and trucks and restored to pedestrians, the city of Munich also built a superior subway system that now connects the restored *Altstadt* with outlying suburban residential districts by means of fast, quiet, and exceedingly handsome underground trains. Moreover, the city also constructed a peripheral highway system to circle the *Altstadt*, thereby keeping through-traffic from penetrating the pedestrian enclave.

In short, Munich's new (and very old) pedestrian inner city was endowed with an infrastructure of transportation systems that serve the people to whom the *Altstadt* belongs — instead of grinding them into the dust. These systems are unobtrusive, invisible, and highly efficient. Without them, the pedestrian inner city probably would not function very well; with them, the pedestrian *Altstadt* is a huge success: its daytime population has doubled since the cars were banned and its businesses are flourishing. And only two years after the initial pedestrian enclave was completed, the city decided to expand its territory to take in the entire medieval center of the town. The decision was made because this most ancient of networks — of nooks and crannies and cobblestoned alleyways — had proved to be the most satisfactory and the most satisfying of urban grids.

Munich is merely the best of the resurrected downtowns to be found primarily in Europe, but increasingly in other parts of the world as well. One or two ancient cities, of course, were never conquered by Detroit. No automobile ever invaded Venice, and so Venice became the Western world's greatest tourist attraction until Disney improved on things a bit by eliminating seasickness as well as gasoline fumes. But now there are many cities that have been liberated, and a few of them have even been supplied with modern infrastructures — subordinate, and kept out of sight — to make them readily accessible to suburbanites as well as ex-urbanites.

To understand what this means in the context of orthodox modern dogma, one must take another look at Le Corbusier's 1925 Plan Voisin for Paris, which proposed to wipe out much of the center of that city in one fell swoop and replace it with a grotesquely monumental graveyard of vast monoliths, strung together by superhighways. In this Final Solution, Notre Dame and the Louvre escaped demolition — barely.

The Munich solution, which has worked remarkably well in human as well as economic terms, is a far cry from the Plan Voisin. Instead of wiping out the heart of their city, the Munich architects and planners decided to reinforce and to reconstruct it, to prop it up with the kind of transportation infrastructure that Disney developed near Orlando. It is a totally different approach to the regeneration of our cities — and a total rejection of modern dogma.

The urban designers of modern Yugoslavia — after a fling with the new Zagreb and similar disillusionments — have rejected modern dogma with similar gusto. They are exceedingly bright and highly responsive to the ways in which people have reacted to the dogmatic modern environments that they, the architects, created initially. And because they have become responsive to the way their friends and neighbors live, these Yugoslav architects have, in effect, broken with the Modern Movement. The one New Town that is most widely discussed throughout Yugoslavia is a place called Split III.

71 **Co-op City, The Bronx, New York. It may never become a tourist attraction.**

Split I is the old city, on the Adriatic; Split II is a new town designed and built in the image of the *Ville Radieuse*; and Split III is a city of streets — a city of pedestrian streets, densely populated, lined with stores, more or less devoid of cars. Its buildings are as modern as anything Le Corbusier designed at his very best. But its spaces are those of the old Zagreb, and of all the other towns from Florence to Walt Disney's Magic Kingdom, that were scaled to people and to their preferred patterns of living.

Several thousand miles away, on the East River in New York, another New Town was going up while Split III was being built. This New Town is Roosevelt Island (formerly Welfare Island), and it is architecturally undistinguished, to put it generously. But the new Roosevelt Island *is* distinguished from most other New Towns built in the United States since World War II by one small and seemingly obvious feature: it has a real street! A real street, with arcaded sidewalks and shops and trees and almost no cars! It is a narrow street, and its walls are eighteen- to twenty-story-high buildings. It crowds you in, perhaps too much so (the height was originally intended to be only twelve stories). But the street has a turn to it so that, as you look down it from either end, you can't quite tell what or who is coming around the bend. In short, it is really a very old-fashioned sort of place. It may be crowded, perhaps overcrowded; and it is unpredictable — full of surprises. And there are balconies that overlook the street, so people can sit and lean out and watch the passing parade.

New apartment towers in Trento, South Tyrol, completed in the early 1970s; and Le Corbusier's vision of a new Buenos Aires, drawn in 1929.

Not long ago, a very neat New Town was built near Toronto, and its architect, a talented and thoughtful man, planned it so that all the apartment towers would face the green, open spaces at the center of the town and partake of their natural goodness. Only one block of apartments — only one out of dozens — faced a nearby superhighway, and try as he would, the architect could not plan his new community without discriminating against that one block of apartments. When the New Town was completed and people began to move in, the "underprivileged" block of apartments — the one facing the superhighway — was fully rented overnight; and the other units — the ones that faced the open spaces and partook of nature — were not fully rented until much later. The reason was quite obvious: prospective tenants preferred to watch the action, even the motorized action; they were not especially interested in watching the grass grow.

We are, in short, rediscovering the street, one of man's earliest urban inventions. The urbanists of the Modern Movement rejected the street when it became an "urban sewer," a convenient right-of-way for everything from babies to trailer trucks. Now that we know, at least in theory, how to restore the street to its original owners, we are learning to restructure our Ideal Cities as well, to turn them into places of intimacy and of interaction rather than into landscaped wastelands of alienation.

Shadrach Woods, who had long been one of Le Corbusier's closest associates, called his last book *The Man in the Street,* not *The Man in the Radiant City*. He obviously had his reasons; he had obviously had his second thoughts. He did not advocate the sort of overcrowding and congestion that characterize many older cities crisscrossed by narrow streets. But he did ask: "Why should quantity exclude quality?" Why, in other words, should the crowding of people (and their favorite activities) be considered deplorable? "Quantity does not exclude quality," Woods wrote, "and more might very well be better than less."

The Fantasy of Mobility

The two most significant urban prototypes produced by the Modern Movement are Le Corbusier's *Ville Radieuse* — towers in a park, spaced far apart — and Frank Lloyd Wright's Broadacre City — every family with its own separate home on its own separate acre of land. Although these two prototypes appear, at first glance, to have absolutely nothing in common, they do share one significant flaw: neither can possibly work without elaborate transportation systems.

Le Corbusier's *Ville Radieuse* could not possibly work without a network of superhighways or of mass-transit lines to connect all those spaced-out towers — unless, of course, he seriously believed that each of those towers might be an autonomous vertical megastructure, self-sustaining and self-fulfilled. But that seems highly unlikely; and so his Radiant City quite clearly presupposed the existence or the creation of a very efficient, high-speed individual- or mass-transit system.

Wright's Broadacre City — a prescription for coast-to-coast suburbia — was even more obviously wedded to the automobile. No really efficient mass-transit system exists now, or is likely to exist in the near future, that can stop every two hundred feet or so — or, for that matter, at two-thousand-foot intervals — without slowing down to a crawl. So Broadacre City could never be realized without the deployment of close to 100 million automobiles. American suburbia, that grotesque caricature of Frank Lloyd Wright's dream, operates on just about that number of cars, and it cannot really hope to function unless propped up by a mobile infrastructure of this magnitude.

74, 75, 76 Monorails zipping through the Contemporary Hotel at Walt Disney World; and through the Lausanne Exposition held in 1964.

74

75

76

Le Corbusier's sketches for his 1925 Plan Voisin for the center of Paris reveal that much of the surface of that Radiant City was to have been occupied by superhighways and by heliports, and that the tiny, disconsolate dots sketched into his projects were supposed to represent people, drifting from nowhere to nowhere. And it is fascinating to read of Frank Lloyd Wright's preoccupation with stately, gasoline-guzzling Lincoln Continentals (painted his favorite red); he clearly considered them the perfect vehicles in which to traverse, circumvent, and frequently escape from his Broadacre City.

In short, it is fascinating, and depressing, to find that modern dogma has, in fact, one built-in constant: decentralization, which *inevitably* leads to hundreds of million wheels, millions of miles of highways, and the wholesale destruction of the natural environment that goes with this.

No one seriously believes that the people who framed the FHA and VA mortgage insurance programs that led to the destruction of millions of acres of the American countryside had ever heard of Broadacre City — but the concept was in the air, as was the concept of Le Corbusier's *Ville Radieuse*, and they had been put there by the great pioneers of the Modern Movement, and by their followers.

The second and third generations of modern architects understood or sensed this: Dr. Reyner Banham, one of the few British critics of architecture and urban design whose prose is clearly intelligible to anyone outside (or, for that matter, inside) the United Kingdom, has said that there is only one way of distinguishing a City of the Future from a palpable fraud: the real thing has a monorail zipping through it; the fraud doesn't.

What Dr. Banham was saying is that the standard image of the Ideal Modern City, as painted by some of the early pioneers (and most of their followers), was that of a huge machine whose moving parts were elements in some smoothly operating transportation system. The elements were not only monorails (although these were the most visible), but also minirails, moving sidewalks, high-speed elevators in glass tubes, conventional subways, and superhighways, helicopters and other aerial conveyances (including ski-lift capsules accommodating a hundred petrified passengers per load), hovercraft, and various kinds of backpack-type attachments designed to render previously harmless pedestrians airborne and, moreover, jet-propelled.

The center of Le Corbusier's Radiant City of 1925: heliport, superhighways, and a thin line of human stragglers.

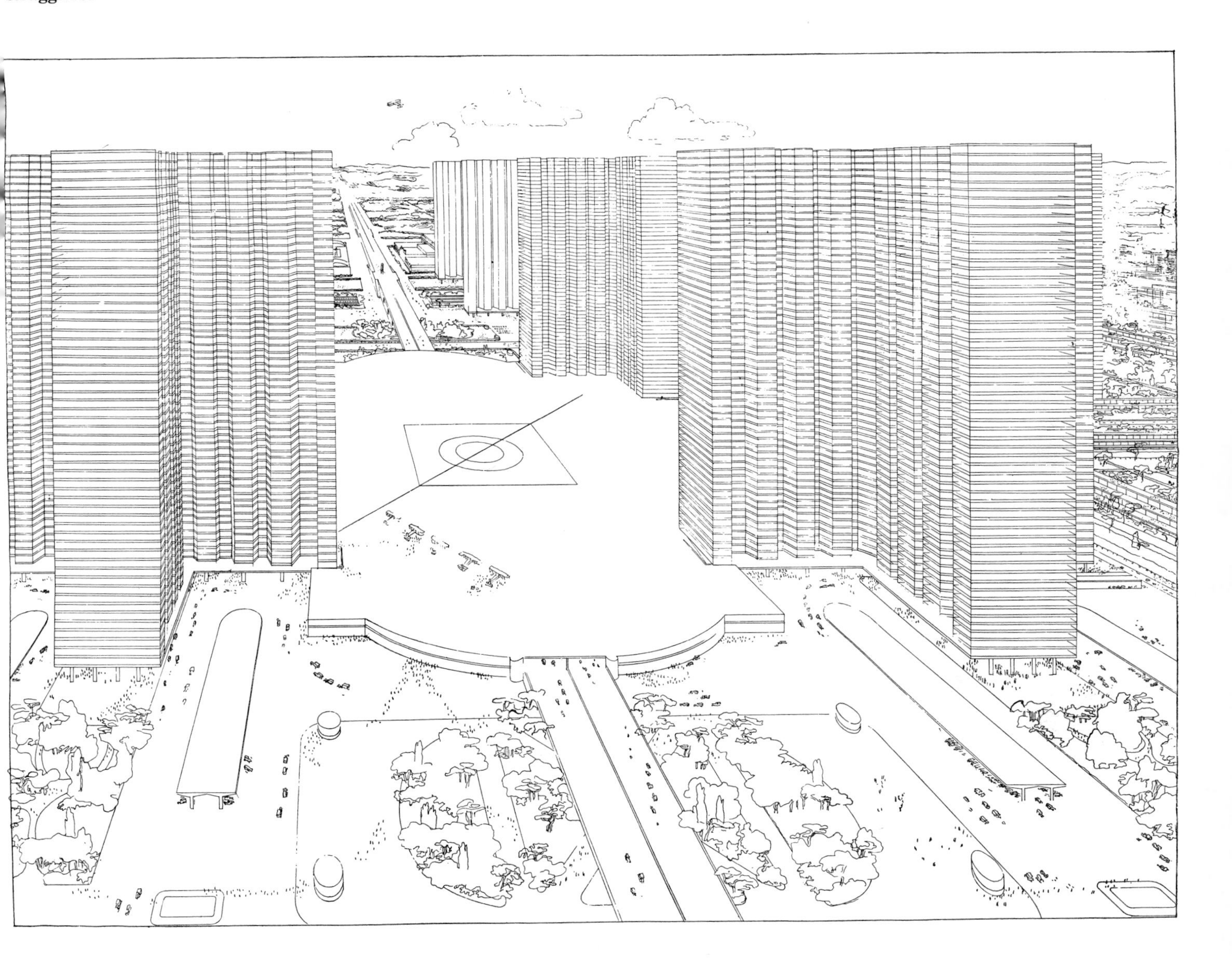

78 François Dallegret's "Space City — Astronef 732" was designed in 1963. It was a proposal to launch 7,000 people on a trip to Mars and (hopefully) back.

78

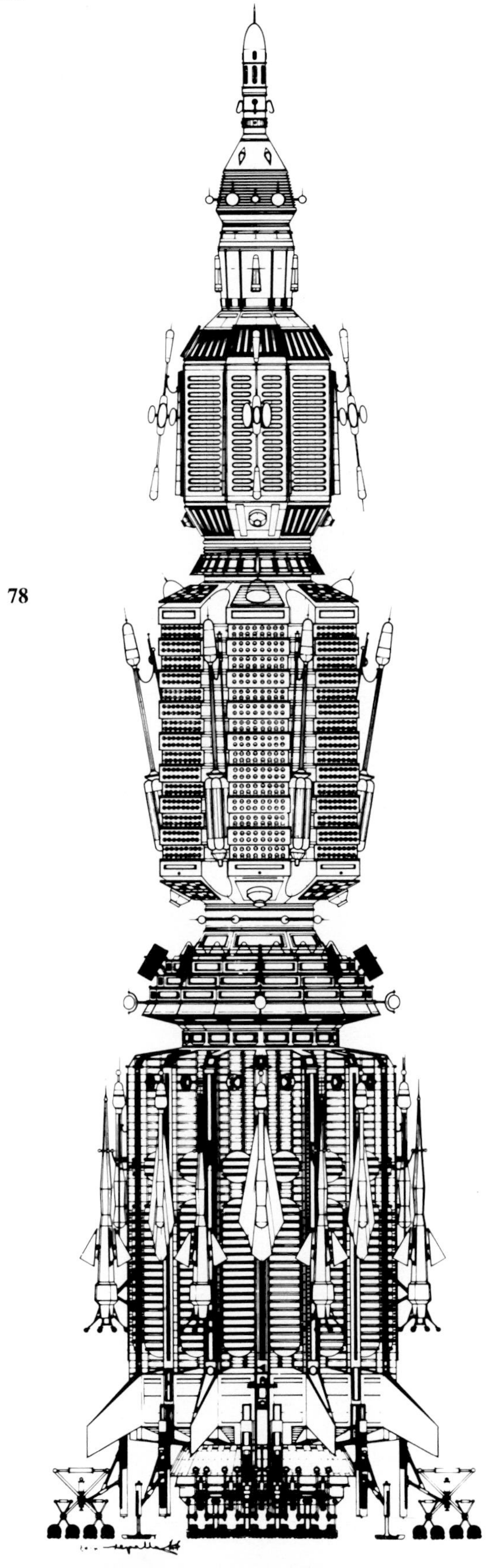

79 The "Walking City," seen here approaching Manhattan Island, is London's Archigram's belated revenge for 1776.

In fact, the only non-moving parts to be found in those giant urban machines tended to be apartments, offices, factories, and other building types that seemed to function better when stationary rather than on the move. That exception, however, was demolished in the early 1960s by that most celebrated of all clubs of modern avant-gardists, the British Archigram group. Archigram's rather remarkable projects included a university-on-rails that could be made to traverse the British Isles (for what reason or purpose was not made entirely clear), as well as a "walking city" that looked like a family of gigantic horseshoe crabs and would apparently be able to walk on water as easily as on land. (One of the startling illustrations depicting this project showed the "walking city" approaching Manhattan from across the Atlantic.)

Preoccupation with mechanized mobility in cities seemed to increase in the 1960s. Archigrammers were fascinated by the space hardware to be found at Cape Kennedy, and they visited the place regularly in the manner of devout Moslems visiting Mecca. The huge gantries and transporters that move the Saturn V rockets from the Vehicle Assembly Building to the Launching Pad were quite properly admired not only for their dazzling engineering beauty, but just as properly because they were structures built on the scale of modern skyscrapers, but designed to move on giant tractors or locomotives! One particularly imaginative designer, François Dallegret of Montreal, proposed a space city in the form of a huge rocket that could be launched into orbit and left there, circling the globe, presumably until such time as things calmed down a bit on earth. And other, more earthbound visionaries of urban design, like R. Buckminster Fuller and Paolo Soleri, exhibited and published their updated Ideal City projects that differed greatly in overall form but had this in common: their inhabitants would be whizzed around in science fiction capsules propelled by anything from rubber bands to rockets.

Mobility is, of course, a perfectly desirable objective, especially if you don't particularly care for your present place of residence and want to get away from it all as often and as rapidly as possible. Thus the poor who are crowded into ghettos see in mobility a means of obtaining better job opportunities for themselves, and better educational and recreational opportunities for their children, in the suburbs. And all city dwellers, poor and rich alike, see in mobility a means of reaching out to nature — as well as of escaping air pollution, noise, and urban tensions, at least on weekends.

But what this really suggests is that the ideal Ideal City would be one that required few, if indeed any, forms of mechanical transportation other than those that every person possesses as part of his or her anatomy. Ideal Ideal Cities, it seems clear, are pedestrian cities: dense concentrations of people and of many varied activities, including good schools, good jobs, and good fun, which will make most mechanical transportation systems rather unnecessary. All the sophisticated transportation hardware that fascinates most contemporary visionaries is not the technology that will fix our urban problems; it is, instead, the mechanical crutch that we need when our cities are in trouble. The ideal Ideal City is a place of crowds and of confrontations, not of highways (or monorails) that are really symbols of alienation. The true Ideal City is a place so jammed with people and events that the only successful criminals are pickpockets, and the only transportation problem is the width of the city's sidewalks — at least until such time as the sidewalks have been leveled and the streets turned back to pedestrians entirely, from wall to wall.

It would be absurd to suggest that mechanical transportation systems should be abolished in their entirety. Obviously, we need them for inter- and intra-urban travel, for the distribution of supplies, for emergencies, and for a great deal more. Still, people seem to prefer individual automobiles or individual feet for mass transit — and not only when mass transit is synonymous with the subway sewers of New York. The gleaming, swift, and elegantly designed Bay Area Rapid Transit (BART) system in the San Francisco Bay region, which was completed in the 1970s, has had serious trouble attracting customers. It was designed to serve about 200,000 passengers a day, but by 1975 only 125,000 had been persuaded to show up. It was designed to be operated by a work force of 1,200, but, again by 1975, with only about 60 percent of the projected passenger load, BART has had to hire 2,000 persons to run its seventy-one miles of track. "One of the lessons of BART," according to a report in the *New York Times,* "is that, all things considered, it seems so far to be an expensive, inflexible and relatively ineffective way to reach and serve the *low-density, sprawling communities* that are typical of American urban expansion since World War II. . . . [In our] residential development . . . there isn't the mass that goes into mass transportation. America, like it or not, has tailored its communities, and its way of living, to the automobile [italics added]." America's communities, knowingly or not, were tailored in that fashion by the two most dramatic urban models advanced by the Modern Movement: Le Corbusier's *Ville Radieuse* and Frank Lloyd Wright's Broadacre City.

In the hierarchy of urban services, transportation systems should rank only slightly above sewers and water mains. The few almost-ideal prototypes of the modern city that have been built in this century are distinguished by the fact that they have invariably relegated mechanized transportation to an often invisible supporting role. The Grand Central complex in Manhattan, for example, is primarily a magnificent pedestrian place of assembly, efficiently and unobtrusively supported by interlocking networks of subways, suburban trains, underground trucking routes, and so on. It is a weatherproof Piazza di San Marco, equipped with an invisible and typically American infrastructure. Rockefeller Center, built twenty years later, isn't quite as successful; still, it is largely an enclosed pedestrian concourse, with occasional glimpses of the outdoors, and again supported by subways and underground service roads. (Initially, it was meant to be plugged into a suburban train system as well.) What makes Rockefeller Center less successful than the Grand Central complex is, significantly, the dominance of the automobile: pedestrians scurry about in artificially lighted tunnels while Cadillacs bask in the sun. In an urban complex built by gas and oil money, this particular pecking order was probably unavoidable and, in any case, symbolically appropriate.

It is interesting to note that the true significance of the neoclassical Grand Central was not recognized for what it was by any of the certified modern pioneers until the terminal was threatened with demolition in the 1950s. Only such impractical geniuses as Antonio Sant'Elia, the Italian Futurist, sensed its significance as early as 1914. And although Rockefeller Center was grudgingly recognized *for its size*, no one seemed to understand its importance as an urban organism until twenty years after its completion. The Museum of Modern Art's influential 1942 primer, "What Is Modern Architecture?," shows a couple of views of Rockefeller Center soaring skyward, but the true meaning of the complex, at ground level and below, seemed to have escaped even MOMA's critical eye. The reason, of course, was the unobtrusiveness of its infrastructure. And unobtrusive it should be, at least that part of any urban transportation network that is mechanized and rapid. It is really part of the plumbing — though not quite as essential.

80 Pedestrian concourse system under New York's Rockefeller Center. It connects all buildings, and joins them to subways, garages, underground trucking services, stores, restaurants, and sunken plazas.

81 Boston's elevated Southeast Expressway (with park bench). The Radiant and Broadacre Cities have destroyed our Center Cities.

81

Unless, of course, you happen to be unfortunate enough to live in one of the Modern Movement's Ideal Cities, in which case the transportation network that links you to job, entertainment, hospitals, schools, shopping centers, and much more is your lifeline; and, in which case, on the day it collapses (as, for example, in the event of a gasoline shortage or a major transportation strike), your life may be literally in jeopardy. At such moments, even the blindest planners begin to see the evils inherent in decentralization — and its inevitable corollary, massive daily population shifts of a magnitude rarely attempted since the biblical exodus, if then.

It may seem unfair to place the blame for urban sprawl upon the masters of the Modern Movement. After all, they did not invent the population explosion, they just tried to respond to it. But the unhappy fact is that their responses were disastrously wrong, and that the sprawling suburbias and the high-rise urban renewal projects built in the images projected by those pioneers have just about demolished the quality of urban life. Only quite recently have the original urban ideals of the Modern Movement been reexamined: in 1963, Serge Chermayeff and Christopher Alexander published their *Community and Privacy,* which blew most of these original ideals sky high. By that time, alas, most of the damage had already been done.

Let no one think that the masters were unaware of the destruction they were planning to visit upon our cities and their people. In 1929, in an article in *L'Intransigeant*, Le Corbusier, that most beguiling of all modern dreamers, wrote one of his great periodic tirades, this one entitled "La Rue." "The street," he wrote, "is the well-trodden path of the eternal pedestrian, a relic of the centuries, a dislocated organ that can no longer function. The street wears us out. And when all is said and done we have to admit it disgusts us. Then why does it still exist?" He obviously thought it shouldn't, and waxed lyrical in describing an alternative vision: "Look over there! That stupendous colonnade which disappears into the horizon as a vanishing thread is an elevated one-way *autostrada* on which cars cross Paris at lightning speed. For twenty kilometers the undeviating diagonal of this viaduct is born aloft on pairs of slender stanchions. . . . When night intervenes the passage of cars along the *autostrada* traces luminous tracks that are like the tails of meteors flashing across the summer heavens . . . the street as we know it will cease to exist."

82 "Look over there! That stupendous colonnade which disappears into the horizon as a vanishing thread . . . the passage of cars along the *autostrada* traces luminous tracks that are like the tails of meteors . . ."

82

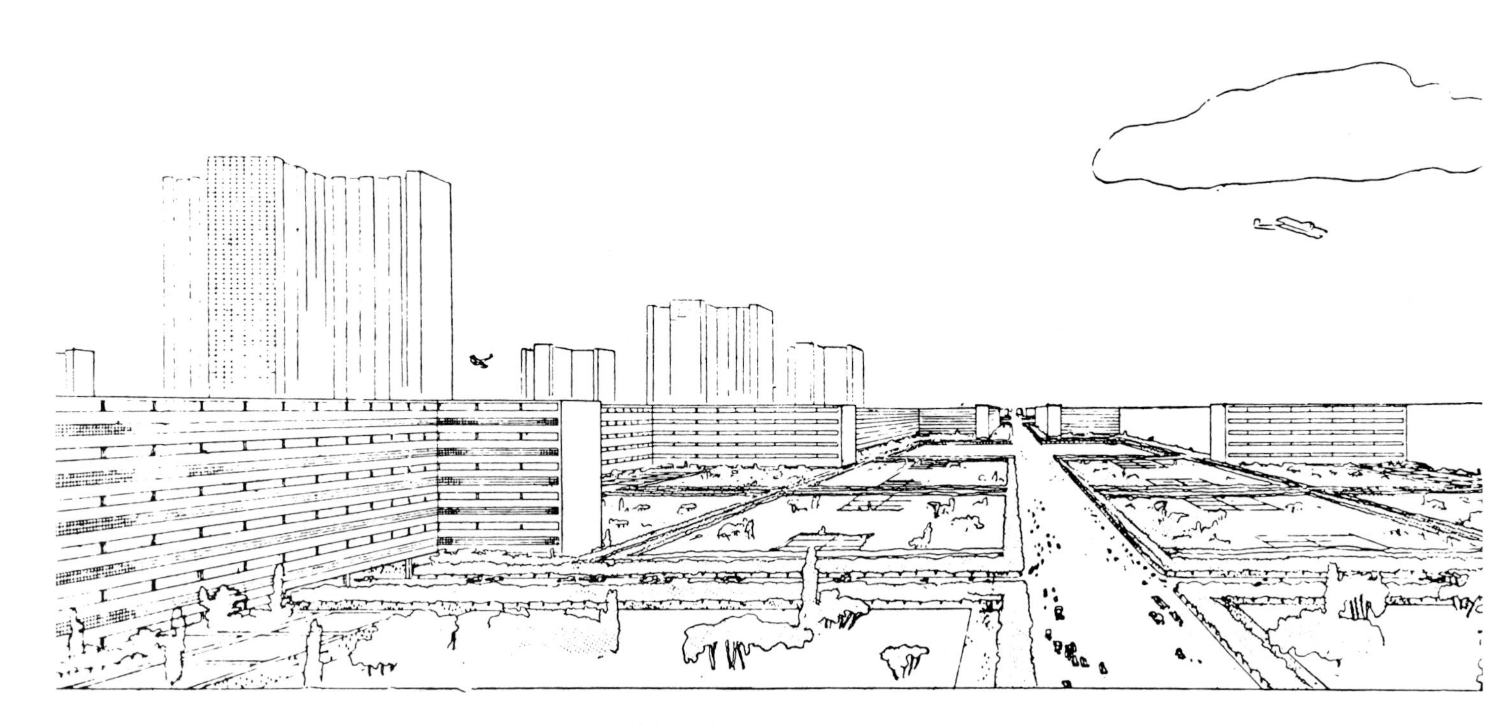

Robert Moses, the megalomaniac highway builder who constructed 627 miles of superhighways in and around New York City, never went quite so far in eulogizing his own masterpieces — nor did he understand their implications quite so clearly.

"The street as we know it" has not ceased to exist completely, though many thousands of miles of it have been wiped off the face of the earth in the name of the Modern Movement. Still, many more hundreds of miles of that "well-trodden path of the eternal pedestrian" remain, and more and more architects and planners of a new generation — a postmodern generation — are determined to revive those well-trodden paths and endow them with a new identity and a new life.

Meanwhile those stupendous viaducts envisaged by Le Corbusier and realized by the likes of Robert Moses may soon join other antiquities on our skylines, like aqueducts, constructed before Western man learned how to stow plumbing and similar necessities out of sight.

The Fantasy of Zoning

83 Zoning diagram of an ideal, functionally segregated city, typical of the kinds of plans developed by planners everywhere in the 1920s and 1930s. This one is British.

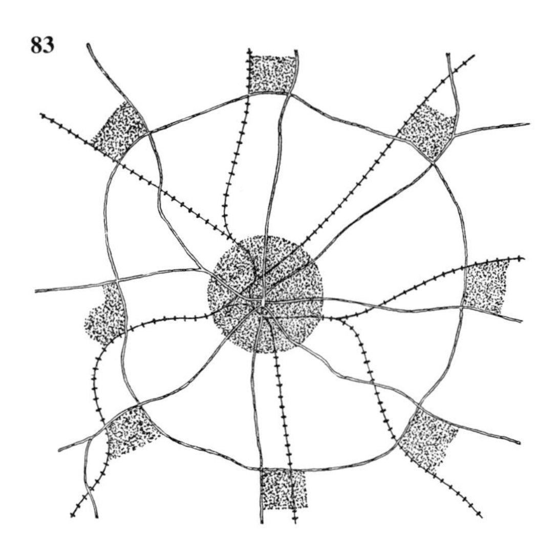

One of the most grotesque urban ideas promoted by the pioneers of the Modern Movement was the notion of zoning a city into areas of different usage.

Residential areas, for example, were thought to be best accommodated among parks and playgrounds, and permanently separated from other urban uses by greenbelts that would be publicly owned and publicly maintained in perpetuity, to protect houses and apartments from various kinds of contamination that seemed to be inevitably attached to industrial or commercial structures. Only a few nonresidential buildings — schools, community centers, and kindergartens — would be permitted to intrude into the otherwise all-residential communities. Even Robert Moses, the New York superplanner, whose disdain for the pioneers of the Modern Movement knew no bounds, used to tell residential communities on Long Island that it was best for them to remain wholly residential — and then some! "Let me warn you against too much enthusiasm for commercializing what nature has given you," he told a Nassau County group in 1945. "Nassau should always be largely residential and recreational. . . . Figure out what sort of people you want to attract to Nassau County. By that I mean people of what standards, what income levels. . . ." The implications were obvious: massive transportation systems would link the Levittowns then being planned to jobs — and to just about everything else.

So, to start with, there would be residential zones. Outside these charming enclaves (and completely separated from them by wide buffer zones) there should be, it was thought, heavy and light industrial districts, commercial areas, cultural centers, health centers, government complexes, and, presumably, zoos. There might also be university enclaves, research parks, and red light districts. Some cities, it was felt, might be large enough to support permanent fairgrounds for commercial and cultural exhibitions; and some might be able to support sizable amusement areas à la Coney Island. All of these districts would, of course, be separated from one another.

84 Le Corbusier's proposal for a city of 3 million inhabitants, advanced in 1922. Zoning usages were segregated in concentric rectangles.

85 Diagram of an "Ideal Communist City," developed by Moscow University planners.

84

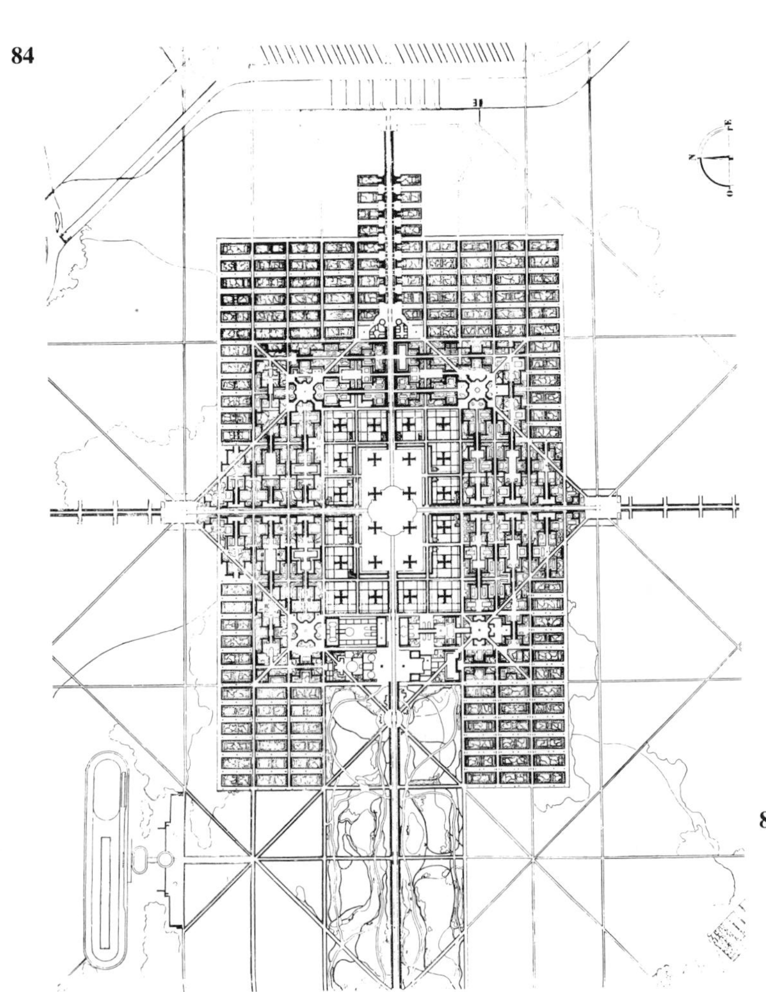

On paper these suggestions seemed eminently reasonable: efficiency of operation might be increased by bunching together structures of similar operational needs, and administrative procedures (like tax assessments, disease control, and other amenities of urban bliss) were probably simplified in the process. Unfortunately, we almost killed off our cities in that process, too. Very few, if any, instruments of modern planning have so successfully destroyed the quality of life in our cities and bankrupted them — and their suburbs and their regions — in the pursuit of some abstract ideal of urban order as zoning did.

The first and possibly the most disastrous effect of zoning was to create neighborhoods that live only a small portion of each day (or week) and are utterly dead the rest of the time. The most dramatic example of this sort of neighborhood is the Wall Street district of Lower Manhattan, which is jammed with people and traffic from 9 A.M. to 6 P.M., five days a week — and is otherwise totally deserted. Others of more recent vintage include the Philadelphia office complex known as Penn Center, which won its planner a prestigious award from the American Institute of Architects as recently as 1976.

85

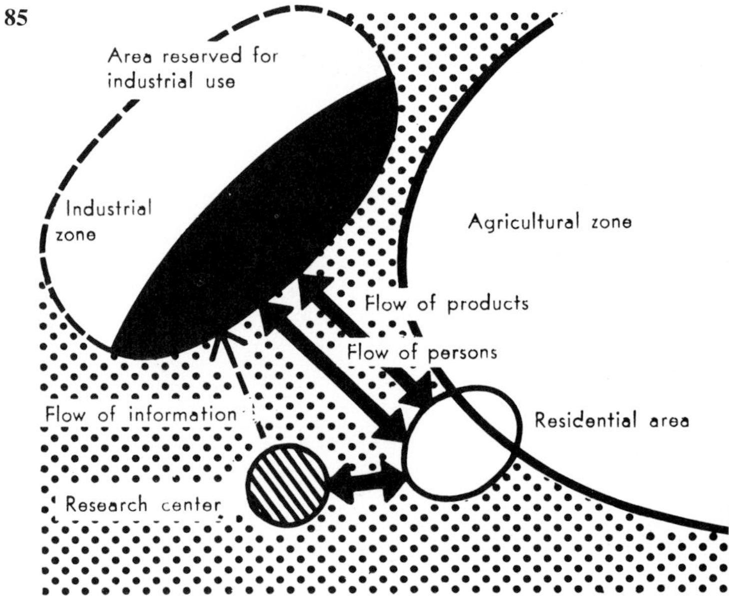

86 Gropiusstadt, in West Berlin — a beautifully zoned residential enclave, without very many pedestrians.

While Wall Street is a lovely and haunting cemetery to visit at night and on its empty weekends, one wouldn't want to live there. It just doesn't seem particularly homey. For many years projects have been designed to breathe life back into those abandoned ruins by building housing along the East and Hudson rivers and on the Battery; but these projects — all of them urgently needed to return Wall Street from the dead — are enormously expensive to realize; for not only is housing needed, but also schools, shops, movie theaters, laundries, nurseries, playgrounds, and much, much more. As it is, Wall Street, thanks to zoning, has almost nothing except office towers and quickie lunch counters.

It is a disaster not only in sociological but also in economic terms. The mammoth transportation systems, public and private, that have been constructed at staggering cost to bring hundreds of thousands to Wall Street (and back home) stand completely idle for more than two-thirds of the time — an incredible misuse and waste of capital as well as of operating funds. The enormous network of power and telephone lines, of steam pipes, of water mains, and of sewers that has been constructed to serve the demands of this part-time community *at its peak hours* stands just as idle when Wall Street's daytime population has decamped for suburbia. No planner, in any area of human endeavor, could professionally survive such a gigantic exercise in waste of human as well as energy resources.

87 Penn Center, Philadelphia — an office complex quite without after-hours activity. The Calder at left was done by the grandson of the sculptor who made William Penn's effigy on top of City Hall.

Indeed, the staggering public investment may very well have bankrupted the rest of the city; for now that this part-time ghetto has been constructed and equipped with dozens of subway lines, superhighways, tunnels, ferries, bus routes, bridges, and thousands of miles of cables and pipes — all of this to serve the "community" for less than a third of the time — the City of New York is virtually bankrupt: it cannot afford adequate mass transit, its utilities are a shambles, and its housing stock is in a state of collapse. As Buckminster Fuller once put it: "The worker goes home to the slum, and the typewriter sleeps with the plumbing." And with the air-conditioning. And with the fluorescent lights, the telephones, the teletypes, the subways, and all the other appurtenances.

Wall Street, and other central business districts like Penn Center, and the monumental waste of our resources that it and they represent, are only the most dramatic, the most visible, examples of the miserable failure of zoning. Less visible but possibly more significant is the human and material waste generated by the creation of residential ghettos that serve our zones of employment.

Suburbia, that vast residential zone which contains more than 30 million little houses on little lots in the United States alone, is the most glaring example. Quite apart from the fact that suburbia and other residential zones are devoid of much life for that part of the day when office and industrial workers have decamped to another zone, the existence of suburbia in the United States accounts for the waste of huge quantities of gasoline.

Dr. Peter C. Goldmark, a pioneer in communications technology, has said that "the single largest use of energy in transportation is in daily commuting by automobile to jobs in the metropolitan areas." This, Dr. Goldmark added, "consumes more than half of our supply of gasoline!" This kind of waste has become even more indefensible with the tremendous strides made, especially since 1940, in the development of communications hardware. It may once have been necessary to assemble hundreds of thousands of office workers from thirty-two counties in New York, New Jersey, and Connecticut within the few square miles south of Fifty-ninth Street in Manhattan on every weekday morning at 9 A.M., and to disperse them on every weekday evening at 6 P.M.; but it makes less and less sense as telecommunications and similar sophisticated systems enable people to work together quite efficiently without having to share the same room, the same building, or even the same city or country. Clearly, this was not predictable when the modern pioneers proposed their neat zoning diagrams, but it became increasingly predictable after the end of World War II; yet the implications for urban forms and urban growth were largely ignored by the planning professions. At this writing, the most significant research into those implications is being carried out not by architects or planners, but by transportation and communications engineers. They are, in effect, trying to repair the damage done to our society by single-use zoning diagrams developed by modern planners — and in trying to repair it, they may complete the alienation process.

But material waste is not the only tragedy, though it is increasingly dramatized by the decline in our energy resources. The waste in human resources as a result of single-use zoning policy is even more devastating. All of us know, from personal experience, the dreadful toll that is taken by the horrors of daily commuting — via highway, or tottering suburban trains. Many of us also know, from personal experience, the sense of isolation from "where it's at" that pervades much of suburbia. This is not said in condescension; it is conceivable that Levittown may someday rival Florence in its human content, if not in physical form. But is it really necessary to wait that long?

It is not. The way to seduce suburbanites to return to the cities they left in haste, fear, or anger is to endow our cities once again with some of the qualities that cities used to have. And the way to do that is to abolish most, if not all, of the zoning patterns that were offered as the prime panacea of urban design by the Modern Movement.

88

88 The daily exodus from Manhattan — office workers returning to suburbia. More than half of the U.S. supply of gasoline is consumed by such commuting from one zone to another.

The most impressive quality that our cities used to possess (before they were sanitized by modern do-gooders) was, quite simply, infinite variety. Within the same city block, sometimes within the same city building, one might encounter apartments, workshops, stores, schoolrooms, offices, studios, places of worship, theaters, warehouses, restaurants, bars, and even governmental outposts. The ideal city block was and continues to be a wild mishmash of disparate activities — a living ''street theater,'' a panorama of men's and women's and children's most interesting preoccupations on a typical day and night. The ideal city block — in terms of life as it is lived, not life as it can be designed — is a capsule travelogue of our time, and of all the times that preceded and helped to shape it. But an Ideal City block, zoned according to modern urban design theory, is an unmitigated disaster.

''The weak point of . . . greenbelt towns,'' the late Henry S. Churchill, an architect and planner, wrote in 1945 in a book he called *The City Is the People*, ''is the failure to provide for local industry and employment.'' He might have added ''entertainment, education, health care, conservation, relaxation, etc.'' Greenbelt towns were and are the most seductive residential zones proposed by the Modern Movement. They are also just about the most boring.

Unhappily, the modern urban designers who are in charge of many rescue operations being mounted in our inner cities think that the way to persuade suburbanites to return to inner cities is to build handsome residential ghettos in or next to our central business districts and enrich them with a school here and a supermarket there. Result: high-rise suburbia, in-urbia, without the essential qualities of Florence, or of certain surviving quarters of New York and London. No would-be defector from suburbia will find such residential ghettos very tempting.

89, 90 Residential zone in New Jersey, and cultural zone in Manhattan. The two sometimes interact — but at vast expense.

89

90

91, 92 New Delhi's Raj Path, designed by Sir Edwin Lutyens and built around 1920. A vast no-man's-land, symbolizing imperial power.

The abolition of single-use zoning patterns is a sine qua non of the resurrection of urban life. Obviously, there are certain kinds of uses — especially certain (but by no means all) industrial uses — that are incompatible with housing and hospital facilities, to name only two. But most uses originally thought to be incompatible have since reached a degree of accommodation via improved technology. So even those horrendous scarecrows conjured up by the original advocates of modern zoning — the steel-mill-next-to-the-maternity-ward kind of thing — are not nearly as scary today as they were fifty years ago, before Jane Jacobs and others reintroduced mankind to the uses of complexity.

Much scarier are certain single-use patterns that have literally demolished the cities upon which they were imposed. One of the most interesting examples of this abuse is New Delhi, whose incredible, bombastic central avenue — the Raj Path — was designed by Sir Edwin Lutyens, the great architect of the declining years of the British Empire. The Raj Path is a dead-straight sweep, surely several miles long, dotted with monuments and crowned with a Viceroy's Palace and other magnificences intended to demonstrate to the heathens what was what. It is an absolutely staggering stage set, requiring only a cast of millions parading two hundred abreast in dazzling uniforms to complete the most stupendous spectacle assembled outside Hollywood.

The only trouble with this magnificent panorama is that it is utterly deserted 99 percent of the time. Near the triumphal arch a few miles from the Viceroy's Palace there may be one snake-charmer entertaining two tourists; on the vast avenue, there may be three vehicles and one jogger; and on the sweeping lawns that line the Raj Path there is often one stout lady, in shorts and T-shirt, doing push-ups.

For, about ten minutes away, by car, is the main street of *old* Delhi, Chandni-Chawk. It wasn't designed by anybody in particular. It just happened. It is lined with stores and workshops and movie theaters and places of worship and, I hope, with bordellos. It is also lined with open-air market stands and with thousands of wall-to-wall people. It is a totally disorganized and frenetic mess. Nobody who has not, in a fit of dementia praecox, plunged into Middle Eastern or Asian street traffic can begin to imagine what goes on at the vortex of Chandni-Chawk. By even the most modest standards of urban design, nothing — nothing whatsoever — even remotely works on Chandni-Chawk; it is, quite simply, an administrative nightmare.

91

92

93, 94 Old Delhi's Chandni-Chawk, designed by no one. Everyone's land — the place where all the city's action is.

Nothing works on Chandni-Chawk, that is, except life itself. For this is precisely the heart of the city, this is the place where all the action is! Whereas Lutyens's grand vision is a vast no-man's-land that divides New Delhi, Chandni-Chawk is everyman's land — a seam that unites rather than divides, a common ground on which all can and do meet rather than an abstract desert of green and asphalt that nobody dares to cross. Except at brief intervals between, say, 3 and 5 A.M., Chandni-Chawk is the very essence of urban life itself: it is everything that people come to cities to experience, everything that suburbanites miss in their splendid isolation.

I have a terrible suspicion that somewhere in the upper reaches of the government of India there sits a thoroughly well intentioned modern planner who, at this very moment, is drawing up a zoning map for Chandni-Chawk, a map that will be its death warrant. The zoning map will undoubtedly designate Chandni-Chawk as exclusively "commercial," and the street will then close down every evening of the week, when the stores close, and open up again in the morning, when those stores open. Garbage collection and deliveries to retailers will be greatly facilitated, as will be the distribution of mail and the passing out of parking tickets. In short, the benign zoning experts will turn Chandni-Chawk into a sort of urban reform school, where they will patiently teach us how to bring order out of chaos — for the common good!

If there is, indeed, such a thoroughly well intentioned modern planner in the upper reaches of the government of India, getting ready to "sanitize" Chandni-Chawk, he or she might like to take a week off to visit New York City, a place massively (and disastrously) "sanitized" several times over in the decades since World War II. The city's innumerable urban renewal projects are everywhere — each one a supersuccess in terms of zoning, and a superfailure in terms of living.

3

94

95, 96 Sixth Avenue, in Manhattan — before and after that particular block was "sanitized."

Only one new community in all of New York City is a dazzling success in human terms, and that is SoHo, the community south of Houston Street that grew spontaneously, in the 1960s, when hundreds of artists moved, quite illegally, into the spacious, cast-iron-fronted loft buildings and created their own spectacular environments without any assistance whatsoever from local city planning authorities.

Now that SoHo is a vibrant, colorful, exciting community — with studios, stores, restaurants, galleries, theaters, apartments, factories, schools, markets, and playgrounds, all cheek-by-jowl, all thoroughly mixed up — the city's planning commission is trying to take credit for its creation. No one, needless to say, is fooled. "Artists driven southward by the redevelopment of Greenwich Village . . . accomplished, without having intended to, what decades of urban renewal had failed to do," said the critic Jason Epstein. "They restored a neighborhood and became its taxpayers." Meanwhile, the official city planners sanctified the accomplished fact by declaring SoHo a "special zoning district," thus obtusely demonstrating, once again, that they had not really learned anything at all. "SoHo's revival suggests that the spontaneous generation which once characterized New York's growth remains a possibility," Epstein pointed out. "Spontaneous generation" is, of course, the very antithesis of planning — and of zoning.

95

96

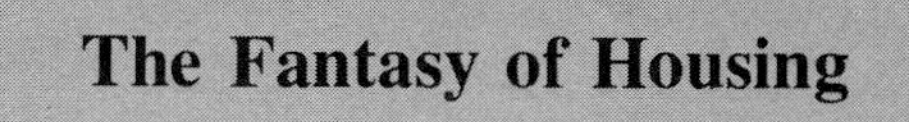

The Fantasy of Housing

97 Design for a housing project done at the Bauhaus in 1928.

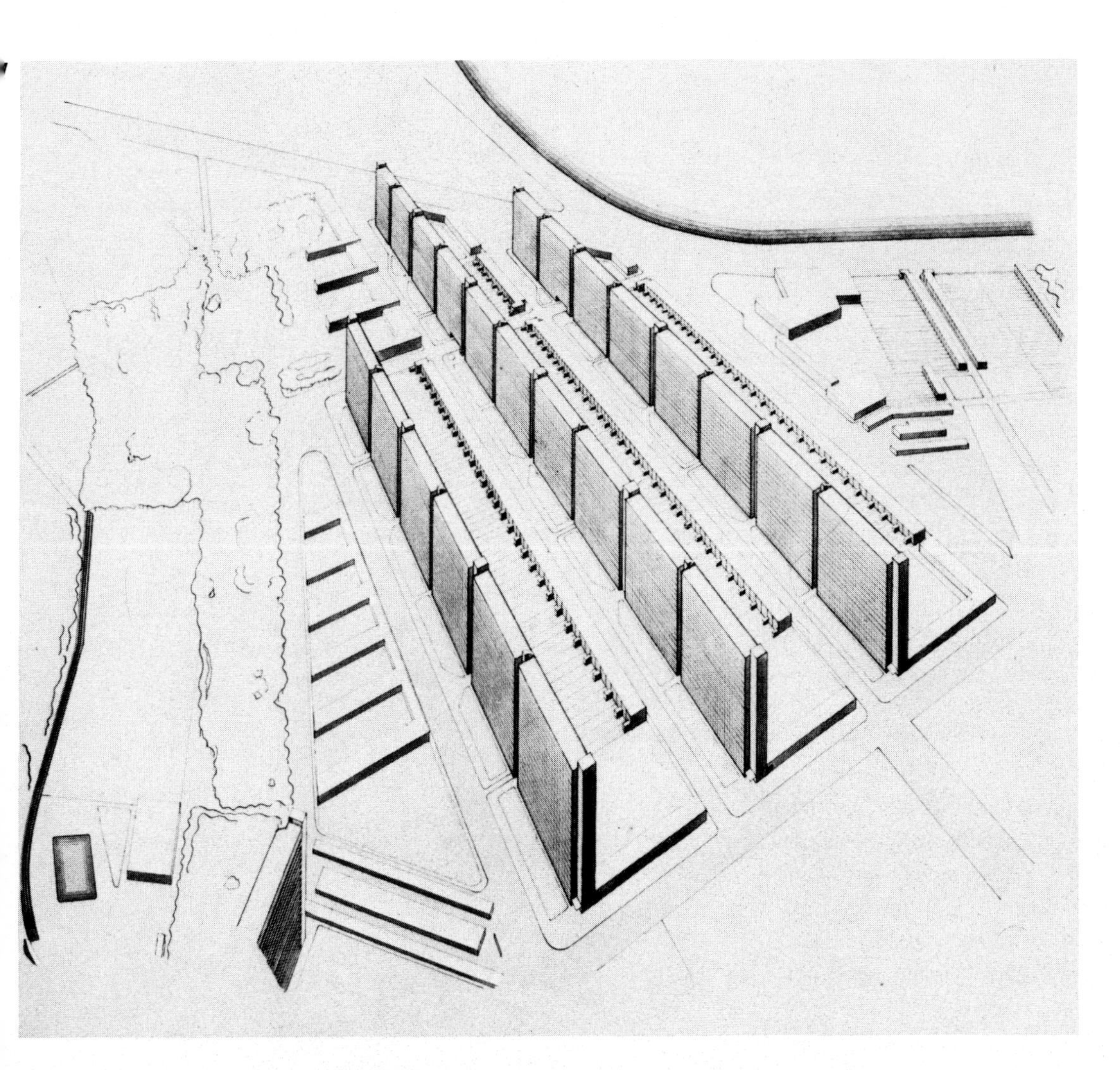

It seems unlikely that the concept of "housing" existed prior to the invention of company towns, army posts, or concentration camps. Prior to the advent of our particular Golden Age, the term would more likely have been "living." It is a gentle term, indeterminate, intransitive, and free; "to house" was not defined at all until very recently — and then as meaning, among other things, "to enclose in a frame [or a] box." "Housing" was not really a very respectable term until the Modern Movement made it so — specifically, when the *Siedlungen* ("settlements") of the Weimar Republic began to enchant do-gooders around the globe.

While the "housing" of company-town workers during the Industrial Revolution was clearly designed to keep them under company control (and out of the rain) — and thus a stable company crop — the "housing" of the *Siedlungen* was just as clearly designed to keep their great-grandchildren under similar control, but this time exercised by trade unions and other forms of workers' collectives. The diagrammatic image of a *Siedlung* would be a more or less idyllic (and more or less geometric) panorama of horizontal or vertical building slabs, from which workers' battalions would emerge each morning to march to the nearest sausage factory, and whence they would return, each evening, ten abreast, to procreate.

That, at least, was the image that the Modern Movement seemed to project. It didn't improve matters when modern housing enthusiasts began to talk about "mass housing" (presumably to go with "mass feeding"); it only made matters slightly more revolting. Nobody not under the control of some bureaucrat or commissar would ever wish to live in a "housing project" (much less a "mass housing project"); nobody not under some such control ever has.

98, 99, 100 Residential zones in Zagreb and Munich, respectively. And terraced student housing at the University of Urbino, in Northern Italy. The latter is a successful effort to create variety.

98

99

100

The original *Siedlungen*, as just suggested, tended to be rows upon geometric rows of concrete slabs into which were fitted more or less ingenious shoebox apartments. On the ground floors these opened into little plots of greenery; on the upper floors there were rows of balconies. On one side the typical housing slab had an access road; on the other there were private and communal gardens. It is not a bad diagram, as innumerable *Siedlungen* all over the world attest to this day. It works especially well for garbage or rent collection, since the pickups (daily, weekly, or monthly) can be efficiently organized to eliminate all wasted motion. It also works rather well for crowd control and other police functions. It is interesting that the diagrammatic *Siedlung* became most popular in (admittedly pre-Nazi) Germany, in the Soviet Union, and in Mussolini's Italy.

To people somewhat less preoccupied with maximum productivity in sanitation and with crowd control than these, it soon became obvious that there was something a trifle inhuman about mass housing diagrams. In the late 1930s, and ever since, attempts were made by certain modern architects in the Scandinavian countries and elsewhere — especially Markelius, Utzon, and the designers of such New Towns as Tapiola — to break up these rigid diagrams and to create more varied patterns of housing. It was felt that a community of mixed age and income groups, though perhaps administratively less tidy, was more desirable in human terms; next-door grandparents, for instance, seemed to make excellent baby-sitters. This in turn suggested that a community of mixed building types was more appropriate than one of identical slabs of concrete, all converging upon the horizon on some ideological vanishing point. High-rise buildings might be appropriate for single people, or even for some elderly couples; row houses or single houses might be more appropriate for families with young children, and garden apartments might work for still others.

The results of such insights produced a number of publicly as well as privately financed communities more interesting in their architecture than checkerboards, and more varied in composition. The Modern Movement's gradual relaxation of rigidity also introduced a certain flexibility in site planning, so that more organic patterns of roads and buildings and parks could be fitted to the contours of the land, and to the condition of existing vegetation.

In fact, the sudden discovery, on the part of the Modern Movement, that man, woman, and child were "human" produced a number of rather self-conscious efforts to design and build communities that would reflect that startling fact. The pendulum swung violently — from the extreme of rigid diagrams in the 1920s to the opposite extreme of man-made chaos in the 1960s. Some architects, like Canada's Moshe Safdie, the creator of Habitat, attempted to combine rigid adherence to a modular diagram with great variety in the final assemblage and with interesting visual results, but with less attractive results for Habitat's financial backers. The human touch — spontaneous or not quite so spontaneous — became the attribute most sought after in modern housing, even in modern mass housing.

It certainly was an improvement over past theory and past performance, but it was not really enough. The fallacy of "housing" lies not primarily in the form of the beast; it lies in the beast itself. The concept of "housing" is, quite simply, a terrible view of the human condition, as Fritz Lang pointed out long ago in his film *Metropolis*. It is also, in the view of theoreticians from Lewis Mumford to Jane Jacobs, a terrible way to create a living city. The excitement found in older cities is, in large part, due to the cheerful chaos randomly built into them: the fact that most of their people, as suggested earlier, live where they work, shop where they live, and educate and entertain themselves and their relatives, friends, and neighbors in those same general precincts.

Obviously, those patterns cannot be translated into the twentieth century without some major modifications. It *may* not be possible to combine houses or apartments with vast assembly-line factories — it *may* not be possible to do so, although nobody has really tried. It *may* not be possible to combine houses or apartments with vast shopping centers — although where some efforts have been made to do just that the results have been extraordinarily interesting, as in the case of the Nordwest-Zentrum, an urban satellite twenty minutes from downtown Frankfurt am Main. And it *may* not be practical to combine houses and apartments with the kinds of mammoth schools that the population explosion seems to demand — although that, too, is being tried on Roosevelt Island, with fascinating educational and social consequences.

101 Residential zone in Southern California. Or, possibly, an army post.

The fact is that mass housing, as a concept, seems to have been employed since the Industrial Revolution as a servant of industry, as a servant of commerce, as a servant of government, and as a servant of bureaucracy. Mass housing is justifiable only because it places a labor force at the manageable disposal of industry; or because it provides a ready and identifiable market for a commercial establishment; or because it justifies employment in ever-growing housing bureaucracies. Mass housing is a very efficient way of providing shelter for a lot of people — very efficient, at least, for those who wish to use large blocks of people for their own benign or nefarious purposes.

Suppose, for the sake of argument, that one started with the proposition that the Ideal City should have no ''housing'' at all of the conventional modern kind, only living neighborhoods of infinite variety; and that all other functions (work, shopping, schooling, and so on) should govern. How would daily life be different?

For one thing, shops might spring up where you really need them — downstairs, rather than at the end of miles of arterial superhighways, in some shopping center surrounded by acres of asphalt on which to park the 250 horses that you need to transport 8 ounces of corn flakes from the supermarket to your kitchen shelf. And if you happen to work in and/or own that store, you might then be living above or next to it, rather than away from it by another daily 250-horse round trip.

For another, if you happen to be a school-age child, your classroom might well be in the same building in which you live, or at worst down the street. And your gym might be around the corner. And another classroom might be upstairs. All this, instead of having to travel miles by school bus, subway, or car to a building that looks as if it might welcome a nuclear reactor, but instead is home-away-from-home to 1,600 kids like yourself who, quite understandably, proceed to vandalize it. If your family hadn't been banished to a housing ghetto, you might actually enjoy school, and come home for lunch, and bring your friends. And your parents might actually use your daytime classroom as a place for parties in the evenings and on weekends — unless, of course, your ''school around the corner'' had become such a great place for you and your young pals to enjoy, seven days a week, that adults would have to find other places in which to meet *their* friends.

As, for instance, in the nearest "museum," which would be located not in some pompous cultural center but in a storefront situation, in a kind of neighborhood automobile showroom, in which the exhibits would be *soft* Cadillacs (by Claes Oldenburg) rather than *hard* ones (by General Motors). This neighborhood "museum" might very well be located in your basement, or even in what used to be your attic. It would certainly not be located in some culture ghetto.

Places of gainful employment might present certain problems in terms of neighborhood integration, but such problems need hardly be insuperable. Offices are just as easily decentralized as they are centralized — in fact, more easily so. Anybody who thinks (as many modern planners do) that it is easier to communicate at shouting distance than at a distance of two hundred miles, say, has not heard of Alexander Graham Bell — or of Dr. Peter Goldmark. The chances are that decentralized office organizations will proliferate as soon as telecommunications become as commonplace in bureaucracies as paper clips. For one thing, decentralized (i.e., small-scale) office space is much cheaper to build; for another, it is much easier to staff well. A neighborhood office can be located in any neighborhood where first-rate help is just around the corner, whereas a centralized, downtown office tower has to attract help from near, but mostly from afar, and the magnetism it must therefore exert becomes increasingly costly. And finally, decentralized, small-scale offices can, of course, be housed in infinitely more pleasant environs — e.g., historic landmarks — and these, suddenly, become much more profitable to maintain and to restore rather than to raze.

102 Educational zone near Los Angeles.

Factories are likely to be a little more difficult to decentralize than offices. One thinks of Detroit and its giant plants, and one despairs of ever being able to integrate such industrial behemoths with a decently scaled, human environment.

And such despair was, indeed, appropriate in the early years of the Modern Movement, when concentration and size seemed to equal efficiency and productivity. But today, in the mid-1970s, it seems not at all impossible that the mass production of consumer goods can be carried on in a way attuned not to the bookkeeper, but to his or her relatives and friends — attuned to the human race.

In Kalmar, Sweden, for example, the rather innovative industrialist Pehr Gyllenhammar (managing director of Volvo) decided in the early 1970s to build a plant in which his cars would be assembled, from prefabricated parts, by small teams of about fifteen men and women working almost like families — as in Gandhi's ideal village-centered industries — to produce highly sophisticated industrial components that would, eventually, coalesce into finished automóbiles. According to Tom Wicker, who reported on the plant for the *New York Times,* "Volvo has at least made a major effort to adapt technology to human beings, rather than subordinating people to the dictates of the assembly line." The obvious consequence, according to Wicker, has been to give Volvo workers some control over the pace of their work and more responsibility. Only time will tell, but the first returns are decidedly favorable.

Automation, combined with increasingly sophisticated telecommunications, will almost certainly separate assembly-line factories into two very different components: first, the relatively small component, in which design and control decisions are made by a few highly skilled individuals; and second, the relatively large component, in which mass production does, in fact, take place.

The first component, Component One — the small, decision-making cell — can easily be located within a small-scale, heterogeneous community and obviously should be; it must attract the best brains, and the best brains tend to gravitate toward a varied and stimulating environment. The second component — the mass-producing one, or Component Two — may soon become entirely automated; it can be located almost anywhere, preferably several dozen feet below the surface of the Mojave Desert, and connected to Component One by means of a sturdy length of cable. So located, Component Two will be able to accept cargoes of raw materials and dispatch its finished products without bothering the neighbors — because there won't be many around to be bothered.

So even a giant industrial plant can be subordinated to the human scale of a natural, crazy-quilt community. This is not merely wishful thinking; it is really an eminently rational alternative that will, sooner or later, appeal to the assuredly rational minds that guide our giant industrial corporations. Once they understand that it is no longer desirable (or especially efficient) to build giant plants and giant housing developments and giant shopping centers and giant superhighways to tie all those giants into knots — and that it is, in fact, infinitely cheaper not to do so — our captains of industry are likely to reconsider. Even though the welfare of their workers may not concern them quite as much as they may claim, the welfare of their stockholders does. Decentralization along strung-out cables that carry telecommunications is a beguiling notion to those who seem to understand the potentials of this new technology as a device to add variety to the human habitat.

To decentralize it, and to mix it up creatively. Our captains of real estate may someday see the light also, though it is likely to take them longer than it will their fellow entrepreneurs. In their infinite wisdom and perspicacity, the captains of New York real estate managed, in the mid-1970s, to overestimate the need for local office space so disastrously that, in Manhattan alone, some 30 million square feet of office space stood, in 1975, unrented and unrentable! Thirty million square feet are the equivalent of fifty Seagram Buildings, and represent a miscalculation worth around $1.5 billion, *not counting the cost of land* or of mortgage payments.

While this rather sizable investment stood unrented, unrentable, and hence empty in Manhattan, and the local captains of real estate were wringing their hands in despair, the city was experiencing a severe housing shortage, a severe shortage of classrooms, and a severe shortage of other facilities. Yet, because "housing" in the minds of contemporary planners (as well as nonplanners) is one thing and education is another, it did not occur to anyone in real estate that it might be possible to adapt some of those 30 million square feet to facilities for which there was considerable demand. Admittedly, it isn't all that easy to convert a typical urban office building into a school or an apartment house or a hospital — or a mixture of all three — but it can be done, and it may even cost less than losing your shirt.

The principal resistance to the abolition of "housing" as a social function is certain to come from the entrenched bureaucracies that have sprung up around the concept. Those housing bureaucracies, like all other bureaucracies, are grotesquely incompetent. In the United States, which specializes in bureaucracy, housing projects built by local, state, or federal agencies invariably cost a great deal more to construct than identical housing units built by private entrepreneurs. A typical "tax dollar" dispatched by a New Yorker, for example, in the general direction of Washington, D.C., will first be collected, analyzed, cross-checked, indexed, etc., etc., by the tax-collecting bureaucracy; next, it will be researched, computerized, and allocated by the budgeting bureaucracy; and finally, it will be brainstormed, breakthroughed, back-fed, cross-fertilized, and otherwise detumesced (and, of course, statisticized) — before it is returned to the public housing authority in the locality whence it came, there to be translated into buildings.

In the course of this scenic round trip, a funny thing is likely to have happened to that original "tax dollar": it may have shrunk to something close to a nickel! Indeed, there are some who claim that truly inspired bureaucracies occasionally manage to shrink "tax dollars" into "minus money" by the time they try to return the cash to its proper owner (the taxpayer) or to the owner's next-door neighbors. When "minus money" is thus generated, the bureaucracies state that their worthwhile programs are dying on the vine because they have been criminally shortchanged or underfunded — and so new taxes are levied in order to realize the dreams that bureaucracy succeeded in squandering.

A further problem is that most governmental bureaucracies in the so-called free world specialize in one, and only one, environmental expertise. There are housing bureaucracies, educational bureaucracies, transportation bureaucracies, health bureaucracies, police and fire bureaucracies, park bureaucracies, and several dozen other bureaucracies. It is fairly simple to build a "housing project"; but it is not at all simple to build such a "project" to incorporate schools, subways, stores, theaters, museums, parks, or police and fire stations — and to get the innumerable, respective "free world" commissars to relate the special programs, the problems, and the budgets to the needs of the community as a whole. Those who, in effect, design our communities do not understand what communities are all about.

103, 104 Residential community in Georgetown, Washington, D.C.; and an award-winning, modern housing project in the same city.

103

104

The government bureaucrats — the only beneficiaries of this sort of nonsense — will not abandon their strangleholds without a bloody fight. Every thoughtful specialist in housing has known for decades that the only decent form of housing subsidy is a rent- or house-buying subsidy coupon to families who clearly need help. Such a subsidy would enable them to select their own places of residence — surely a socially desirable objective, likely to generate (or conceivably to discourage) the sort of mix that may or may not be the democratic ideal. In any event, self-determination. Such subsidies could be handled at any governmental level, preferably the lowest, thus eliminating vast overlays of bureaucracy. They would encourage private building, demonstrably much more efficient than governmental building. And they would tend to generate much crazy-quilt construction (and living) of the sort that made our older cities "ideal."

But this kind of self-determination in the selection of a citizen's place of residence would, quite obviously, put an awful lot of bureaucrats out of business. (It would also make it exceedingly difficult for superplanners to draw up their diagrammatic *Siedlungen* in which to make the rest of us happy.) The incredible wastefulness of present procedures, and the utter failure in human, economic, political, and plainly practical terms of centralized housing and planning operations, will inevitably lead to the abolition of these bureaucracies.

So the facts of life — or, at least, the realities of the political marketplace — are quite likely to suggest certain changes that can only help to improve life in cities. It will not come a moment too soon. Aristotle wrote, in his *Politics*, that "men come together in the city to live. They remain there to live the good life." He did not say that men come together in the city to be housed, or to be educated, employed, elevated, exploited, policed, or governed. He wrote "to live"; and he added that they remained there "to live the good life."

105 Housing development in West Germany.

Some of the educators of the Modern Movement took a rather dim view of the teaching of history, and so one assumes that Aristotle was not on the Bauhaus reading list. Too bad; his writings might have saved all of us a fair amount of trouble. For Aristotle, according to Lewis Mumford, brought to the discussion of cities "a knowledge of the immense variety of species and an appreciation of the endless creative manifestations of life itself. . . . For Aristotle," Mumford said, "the ideal [city] was not a rationally abstract form to be arbitrarily imposed on the community; it was rather a form already potential in the very nature of the species. . . ."

It is clearly unfair to blame the Bauhaus exclusively for creating "rationally abstract forms to be arbitrarily imposed on the community." One of the grandfathers of the Modern Movement — even of the Bauhaus (though he was passionate in his hatred of industrialization) — was John Ruskin; and it was his view that "the first duty of a State is to see that every child born therein shall be well housed [*sic!*], clothed, fed [*sic!*], and educated." To achieve this, Ruskin believed, "government must have an authority over the people of which we now do not so much as dream." However admirable Ruskin's social conscience may have been, what a dim view he held of a free society!

The Fantasy of Form

106 Rietveld's "Steltman Chair" was designed in 1964. It was, apparently, available in both left- and right-handed versions.

)6

The pioneer Modernists of the 1920s had a very difficult time finding clients who were willing to commission them to design buildings of any significant size. Le Corbusier, for example, built hardly more than two dozen small houses or projects during his first ten years as an architect. Mies van der Rohe built even fewer. Frank Lloyd Wright barely managed to survive during some of the years between the two world wars, and Walter Gropius and Marcel Breuer did their most voluminous work after World War II, making their living in the 1920s and 1930s largely by teaching a younger generation of students how *they* might survive if *they* became architects.

Partly because of this dearth of more substantial work, the pioneers of the 1920s concentrated much of their energy on furniture. The resulting twentieth-century revolution in furniture design was almost entirely the work of some half-dozen architects — most specifically that of Marcel Breuer, Le Corbusier (and his collaborator in those early years, Charlotte Perriand), Ludwig Mies van der Rohe, Alvar Aalto, Gerrit Rietveld, and, to some degree, Frank Lloyd Wright — and including, much later, the work of the architects Eero Saarinen and Charles Eames. No really significant innovation in furniture design and furniture technology was made in those years — or, for that matter, since — by "interior designers" or by traditional craftsmen.

107 Two of Frank Lloyd Wright's polygonal chairs, designed to fit the polygonal module of some of his houses.

107

What made the work of these architects so significant was that their chairs and tables and cabinets were intended to relate directly to the spatial problems and opportunities inherent in the new architecture. For example, the transparent, tubular steel furniture invented by Breuer and others was intended to reinforce the notion of the open plan, with its visual and actual flow of space — and, as we have seen, with its considerable drawbacks. In fact, such furniture tends to look more than a little lost in the very few grand spaces that we can sometimes still afford to construct, but it looks entirely to scale in more modest environments.

The modular storage units designed by these same architects were dimensioned to fit into the modular plans of modern buildings — and the drawbacks that modular planning seems to possess. The strange, often polygonal chairs and tables designed by Frank Lloyd Wright related closely to his rather bizarre triangular, rhomboid, or hexagonal planning modules, and so on. (The massively overstuffed furniture designed during those same years by ''modernistic'' decorators in France, the United States, and elsewhere — now often referred to as Art Deco — bore no relationship to the spacious and airy architecture of the Modern Movement at all; but the furniture designed by the pioneer architects quite clearly did.)

Even some of the more esoteric furniture developed by architects like Gerrit Rietveld bore a direct relationship to the architectural and aesthetic problems of the time, at least as he saw them; he was a member of De Stijl, the Dutch group of artists and architects that came to the fore around 1917 and continues to influence much of modern art and architecture to this day. Rietveld's houses were spatial elaborations on themes developed by Piet Mondrian, Theo van Doesburg, and other artists of Mondrian's circle; and Rietveld's furniture was entirely at home in that environment.

8 Chromium-plated chairs (vintage 1928) by Le Corbusier and Charlotte Perriand. In back, a traditional Victorian Chesterfield sofa, from which to observe the chairs in comfort.

So far, so good. There has always been a degree of consistency in the range of objects produced by any given style: the natural forms — plants, sea shells, bones of animals, and similar flora and fauna — that formed the inspiration of the Art Nouveau style are clearly visible in the buildings of Antoni Gaudi in Barcelona and of Baron Victor Horta in Brussels; in the furniture of Hector Guimard and in his entrances to the Paris Métro; in the glass by Louis Tiffany in America; and in the posters of Toulouse-Lautrec and the paintings of Van Gogh. Wherever you looked, these same swirls and whiplash curves revealed themselves as organic parts of a structure, as applied ornament, or as the themes of a drawing or a painting.

Consistency in a given style, then, is nothing new. But the consistency found in certain artistic manifestations of the Modern Movement seems, to put it mildly, a bit arbitrary. One may admire a two-dimensional abstraction by Piet Mondrian without necessarily wishing to recline on its three-dimensional elaboration; and one may admire a Suprematist Composition by Kasimir Malevich without necessarily wishing to cuddle up with it. One of the differences between the style of the Art Nouveau and that of the Modern Movement is that the former was insistently naturalistic, organic, and humanistic; whereas the latter was and is just as insistently and consciously abstract, geometric, mechanistic, and synthetic. Thus the former, quite clearly, lent itself to translation into forms attuned to the human anatomy — often to the point of sentimentality, whereas the latter does not.

There is no question that much of the "classic" furniture that came out of this radically — and rationally — creative period of design is ravishingly beautiful. I have long owned chairs by Breuer and by Le Corbusier and Charlotte Perriand, and they are marvelous examples of what New York's Museum of Modern Art has called Machine Art.

The Le Corbusier/Perriand version of the traditional so-called British Officer's chair, for example, is an object of absolutely dazzling perfection, easily on a par with the best work by Ettore Bugatti or by Constantin Brancusi: it is a construction of chromium-plated tubes in straight lines and quarter-circles, with elegantly accentuated connectors and sharply pointed conical finishing plates — an object as sexy as the sassiest sports car. The tubular steel structure supports various wide and narrow straps of cowhide or of plain leather held in tension by tight wire springs; and the combination of all of this is an everlasting pleasure to behold.

8

109 Profile of Verner Panton's 1960 plastic chair. It also stacks.

110 Rietveld's "red-blue chair" of 1918. A very interesting construction in the manner of Mondrian.

It is not, however, an everlasting pleasure to besit. In fact, this particular chair, and others of its vintage by these and other designers, appears to be a boon primarily to chiropractors. They hold the human frame as if in permanent traction; they bruise the human skin each time one skirts too closely to them; their exposed steel springs, nuts, bolts, clips, and other industrial fastening devices are guaranteed to shred the most durable of miracle fabrics. And stockings and slacks unravel when brought within mere proximity of the Work of Art.

And that, quite often, is not all; some of the most beautiful chairs of those early years have a disconcerting way of expelling their occupants tableward by tilting forward in an unexpected, avant motion caused by the smooth curves of the tubular and rounded metal or plywood legs where they make contact with the floor. Others — especially those insistently form-fitting lounges that support the spine in something fairly close to the immediate post-fetal position — are exceedingly difficult to dismount without resort to block and tackle. Still others — such as those with seats of smooth, bent, or molded wood or plastic — tend to eject their occupants more gently, but quite as effectively, in the manner of a playground slide.

109

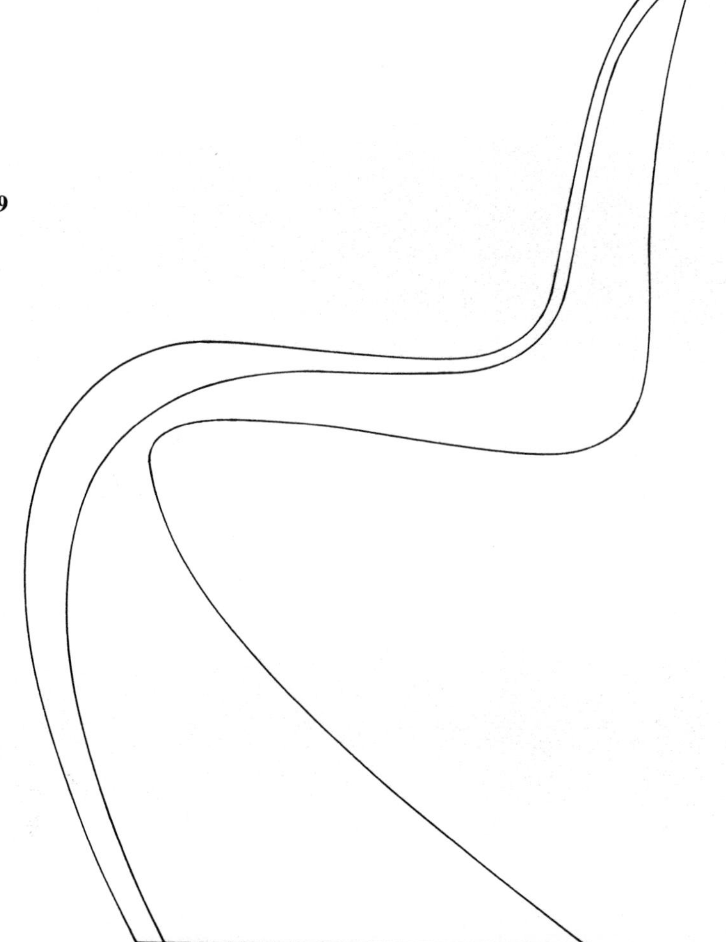

1 Rietveld's "Berlin chair" of 1923. The De Stijl painter Huszar supplied the color scheme — several shades of gray.

112 Russian constructivist chair by Vladimir Tatlin, designed in 1927. Tatlin was interested in aerodynamics.

And finally, there are some chairs of this period that cannot be easily abandoned without the help of an orthopedic surgeon: a justly famous Work of Art by Gerrit Rietveld, known as the *Rood-blauwe Stoel* ("red-blue chair") of 1918, is an ingenious trap worthy of the most skillful elephant hunter. The chair, according to the Australian sculptor and designer Clement Meadmore, "appears to be made solely according to aesthetic criteria . . . the functional aspect appears to be incidental. Rietveld himself is said to have complained of bruising his ankles on it, and a certain daring seems required actually to use the chair."

Even more daring was called for five years later, when Rietveld designed what has become known as his "Berlin Chair." That one also called, alarmingly, for some major genetic changes in the human race, for it was entirely asymmetrical: it appeared to assume that people's *left* arms were mounted onto their bodies at an elevation approxitely six inches above their *right* arms, and that their right legs were endowed with some kind of universal joint or ball bearing located within the knee, and designed to permit the lower *right* leg to be either unhinged or swiveled sideways rather like a windshield wiper gone berserk. A couple of years later, the eminent "Russian Constructivist" Vladimir Tatlin created a chair made almost entirely of tubular steel spaghetti. "He was deeply involved in the making of flying machines," Meadmore reports. His 1927 chair was, clearly, part and parcel of that involvement: it required little more than a seat belt to reassure its occupant that he or she would survive whatever turbulence might be generated by the "graceful, swooping, organic form that," according to Meadmore, "Tatlin . . . designed."

110

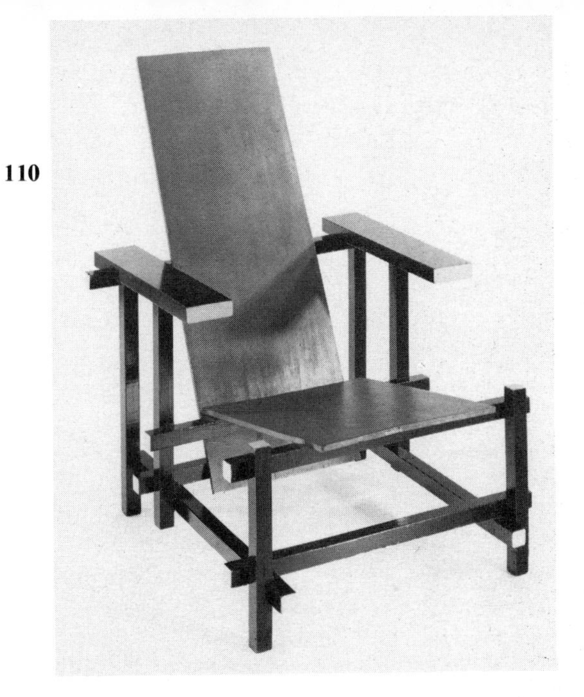

111

112

113, 114 Rietveld's Zig-zag chair of 1934. It speaks for itself — though not, perhaps, for the human anatomy.

114

The Modern Movement's love-hate relationship with the human anatomy reached some sort of climactic crisis in 1934, when Gerrit Rietveld designed and made his Zig-Zag Chair, presumably for "zig-zag men" and "zig-zag women." It is an extraordinary piece of work, strongly reminiscent of Shaker furniture in America; like the Shakers, Rietveld seemed to feel that there was something rather sinful about wanting to sit down — thus the would-be sitter should be made to suffer.

The Zig-Zag Chair is what its name suggests: a construction of four planes of plywood zigging and zagging up from the floor (where the first plane lies flat) to the back support, three zags farther up. In between, there is a razor-edged seating slab that appears designed to sever whatever arteries are located within the hollow of one's knee; a formidable back slab appears designed to dislodge any vertebrae insouciant enough to make contact. "The Zig-Zag is a small chair," according to Meadmore, "and it appears poised, almost as if alert to its task." The description is accurate — and ominous.

When a modern furniture or industrial designer is asked to define his job, he will usually say that it is "problem solving." This is a noble objective, of course, but not one that has been attained with notable success by the pioneer designers of the 1920s, or by many of their successors to the present day.

If the "problem" of modern furniture design is to cause a minimal interruption in the visual flow of interior space, then the transparent chairs and tables designed by Mies van der Rohe and Le Corbusier are indeed inspired solutions — though Marcel Breuer's proposal for an ideal "chair of the future," advanced in the 1920s, probably takes the cake. He thought that such an ideal chair should be entirely invisible — i.e., a compressed air jet, emanating from some secret nozzle, randomly embedded in the floor, on which the sitter would then teeter in minimal abandon.

If the "problem" of modern furniture design is to supply visual delight — i.e., a work of constructivist art, at a bargain price — then those same transparent chairs and tables (long and quite properly certified as Works of Art by New York's Museum of Modern Art) do, indeed, offer solutions that delight the eye: no sculpture by Brancusi outdazzles a chair or a table by Mies van der Rohe, and no construction by El Lissitsky outzips that chair of mine by Le Corbusier and Perriand.

113

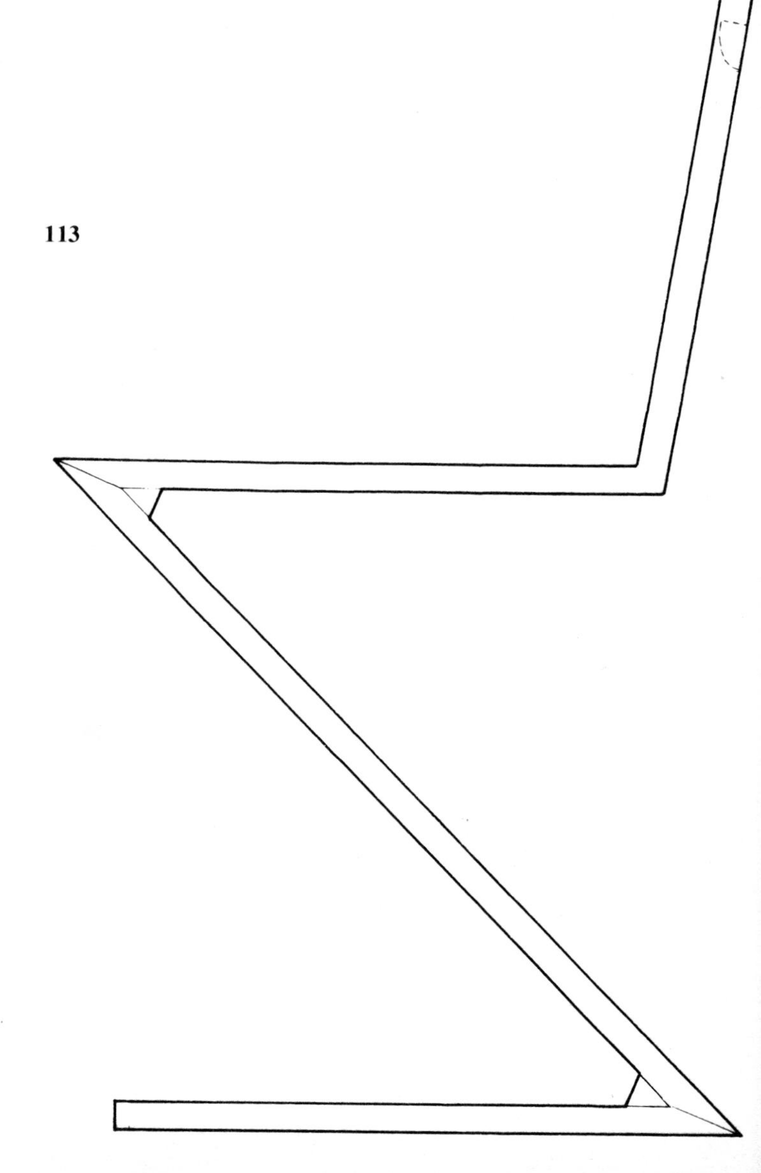

115

115 Bauhaus lighting fixture, 1925. Chains will hold the glass globe while the electric bulb is being changed.

116

116 Faceless watch, designed to keep its wearer guessing.

But if the "problem" that cries or whimpers for solution is simply how to sit in comfort, and drink and eat and store your shirts in comfort, then these works of constructivist art seem to leave a thing or two to be desired. Men and women do not live by bread alone, nor do they, presumably, sit exclusively on Barcaloungers; but neither do they sit, with notable abandon, on razor edge, steel spring, chromium tube, Lucite, asbestos, polished plywood, or tempered glass — or, for that matter, on tensioned horsehair. The truth is that the way to enjoy much of the furniture bequeathed to us by the Modern Movement is to observe it from a safe distance while ensconced in overstuffed chairs or in plush bargain-basement sofas; and the way to enjoy navigating among the hard-edged tabletops is to wear shinguards to fend off the problems "solved" by glass-topped coffee tables, and to wear upholstered bustles for fending off the problems "solved" by razor-edged dining tables and modular cabinets.

So much for minor lacerations. Because of its dedication to visual asceticism and purity, the Modern Movement insisted also upon the use of "honest products" and "honest materials," "honestly" deployed. Lighting fixtures tended to be stark, probably conducive to the early formation of cataracts. Drapery and upholstery fabrics and rugs had to be uniformly oatmeal, a color scheme not too likely to inflame the senses. Hardware — doorknobs and such — was designed in that same Calvinist Machine Art idiom that distinguished those zippy, constructivist sitting machines: they seem designed to elevate the spirit while simultaneously skinning your knuckles. And the hard, metallic, plastic (or merely crystallic) walls, floors, and ceilings that must form the backdrop to this surgically pure environment were an acoustic disaster, not unlikely to cause severe brain damage in the short or long run. (Wherever possible, wall surfaces had to be dead white — a lovely color, easily maintained so long as the consumers of this pure environment always wore cotton gloves or had had their fingerprints erased by plastic surgery.)

Similarly purist approaches to "problem solving" were applied to the design of objects other than chairs and tables. At the justly famed Bauhaus created by Walter Gropius at Weimar and, later, at Dessau in the years following World War I, designers applied their "problem-solving" talents to the creation of everything from a soup spoon to a type face. Alas, the preoccupation with cubist aesthetics — the *true* motivation of those talented Bauhaus men and women, though they would never admit it — got in the way: sharp-edged, cylindrical, conical, or hemispherical metal containers do not connect terrifically well with the human anatomy (and are not easily cleanable, if the truth must be told); surfaces of dazzling polish lose much of their dazzle after the first scratch on the polished Machine Art surface, and all of it after the second or third. The lovely Bauhaus sans-serif type faces that swept the modern Western world (and continue to dominate modern graphic design to this day) turned out to possess one disconcerting flaw: they were (and continue to be) much more difficult to read than the traditional Roman letters.

117 Cubist chess set, designed in the 1960s. A dazzling assemblage of minimal sculptures, conveying a minimum of information.

The Bauhaus spawned more Good Design than any one breeding ground established or identified in this century. Among the products developed by its masters and students were not only unsittable chairs, back-breaking beds, and unreadable type; there were also many of those educational toys that our children hate; water pitchers that titillate your visual perceptions while wetting your pants; coffee-making machines ("designed for mass production") so complicated as to make one want to switch to tea; a "samovar with spirit lamp and small pot for tea essence," consisting of so many grotesque cubist, pre-cubist, and post-cubist movable (and static) parts that you might want to switch back to coffee; and finally, a whole series of floor, wall, and ceiling lamps designed by someone who had obviously been maddened in real life by the problem of replacing a light bulb: the solutions would have warmed the heart of El Lissitzky, and blown every fuse in the neighborhood.

Form, in short, seemed to conquer content. Today, on the shelves of the innumerable "modern design" stores around the world, we find the descendants of these labored efforts at "problem solving": modern clocks and watches that captivate the eye, but do not tell the time (because their faces have no numbers, and sometimes no hands); modern calendars that will not reveal today's date unless backed up with information supplied by a conventional diary — but that do, admittedly, spell out something in a new and ephemeral Language of Vision, though not one of Comprehension; and modern graphic symbols that do, indeed, acquaint the masses with the work of that great and round-edged cubist painter Fernand Léger, but unhappily do not acquaint the masses with very much else in the way of information, e.g., how to locate the nearest john. And then there is that absolutely splendid example of modern, Machine Art "problem solving": a chess set designed by one of the finest cubist artists of our day and machined impeccably of stainless steel, whose pieces, alas, are virtually indistinguishable from one another by the naked or even the hooded eye. Clearly, the end of chess.

Illegible but impeccable typography; unintelligible but impeccable timepieces and calendars; unsittable but impeccable chairs; uncleanable but impeccable spoons; intolerable but impeccable sound and light; untouchable but impeccable glass, plastic, marble, and chrome. ''We reject the tyranny of form,'' the modern masters used to say. Content — or ''problem solving'' — was the name of their game. Quite so; but the problem that the Modern Movement really wants to solve, judging by its performance to date, is the infuriating anatomy of the human race: nothing, dammit, is going to function — Bauhaus-wise — unless all men are redesigned as cubes, and all women redesigned as spheres. Once that is accomplished, everything else will fall into place with a barely audible click — and the solution will then become the problem.

The Fantasy of Architecture

Protest in Boston, in the 1950s.

Around the turn of the century Daniel H. Burnham, the Chicago architect who became one of the folk heroes of the Modern Movement (although he had, in fact, been a devotee of the École des Beaux-Arts), laid down the law that would govern modern architecture and urban design for the next seventy-five years. ''Make no little plans,'' Daniel Burnham said. ''They have no magic to *stir men's blood* and probably themselves will not be realized. *Make big plans*; aim high in hope and work, remembering that *a noble, logical diagram* once recorded *will never die*, but long after we are gone will be a living thing, asserting itself *with growing intensity*'' (italics added).

119, 120 Brasilia, the final solution.

119

120

Seventy-five years later Professor Marshall Berman, the political scientist, wrote that "it seems virtually impossible today to feel or even to imagine the joy of building, the adventure and romance and heroism of construction. The very phrases sound bizarre. . . . How have we come to condemn the process and the products of construction as emblems of everything we find most destructive . . . massive ugliness, sordid venality, outrageous windfalls of wealth, endless storms of dirt and noise, big plans laying waste little people's lives, organized viciousness without redeeming social value?" And in that same year E. F. Schumacher wrote, in a book whose title would become famous, that "small" was "beautiful." Not *big* plans, *small* plans. He went on to say that there was something inherently "beautiful" about planning and designing on a small, human scale — and something even more beautiful about not planning at all. "A plan is the result of an exercise in the freedom of choice," Schumacher wrote. "The choice has been made; all alternatives have been eliminated . . . [people] have chosen *to surrender their freedom* to act otherwise than prescribed in the plan" (italics added). The Modern Movement has marched, unerringly, along this straight and narrow path, from Burnham to Le Corbusier's Plan Voisin to Robert Moses and the "urban sanitizing" popular in West Germany after World War II. People throughout the developed world "shrink back in fear and loathing" — as Professor Berman put it elsewhere — whenever a new project raises its head. It is a devastating tragedy to anyone dedicated to the fundamentally decent intentions of the Modern Movement that those fundamentally decent intentions almost invariably arouse "fear and loathing" in the community.

Somehow, without apparently being aware of what they were doing, the masters and their followers in the Modern Movement have become advocates and promoters of ugliness, of venality, of greed, of social disintegration, of land exploitation. Wherever and whenever they take a public stance, it is almost invariably on the side of the aggressors — arguing for the destruction of a well-established neighborhood; arguing for the construction of a mammoth skyscraper (or two, or ten) that will be environmentally and visually polluting, and quite possibly dangerous to your health; arguing, earnestly, that being ground into dust by a bulldozer is, in fact, good for you; and that being blinded by glare, deafened by "white" noise, frostbitten by downdrafts, seared by updrafts, and lacerated by contacts with hard-edged environmental components will, in fact, elevate your visual and tactile literacy, and your spirit. And arguing, finally, that the new technology is also very good for you — even if it saturates the air with asbestos flakes, rust, and falling glass, and even if, to add insult to injury, it then bankrupts you in the bargain.

How on earth did architects — idealistic ombudspeople for the environment — manage to paint themselves into this ridiculous corner? Greed was certainly one factor — though most architects die poor; it is the developer, contractor, manufacturer, realtor, and building trades unionist who profit from construction. So the real reason is clearly something unrelated to monetary reward; the expected reward for grinding your neighbors into the dust is to be found in heaven, or in history: the Modern Movement, with its shining dogmas, its exciting slogans, and, above all, with its absolute self-righteousness, was and is, quite clearly, a religion as irrational as all others, from snake-handling to psychoanalysis. Like all religious cultists, the members of the sect treat their critics with patient condescension: those who don't want to be ground into the dust (or snake-bitten, or shrunk) don't know what's good for them; but the cultist, to whom the Truth has been revealed, *does* know, and he or she will ram the new Language of Vision down the nonbelievers' throats, even if they gag on it.

The cult is doubly seductive in that it not only insures the believer a place in heaven, but also a more or less permanent place on earth. No other profession leaves such large and eminently visible monuments to itself (and to its clients). To be an architect is to achieve a degree of immortality; to be a megalomaniac architect is to achieve a *high* degree of the same. As Frank Lloyd Wright once said, "Doctors bury their mistakes, but architects can't." Their mistakes (as well as their successes) live on with them, *but mostly after them*. The result is immortality.

The promise of immortality is no longer as beguiling as it once was — and it has never been a very interesting subject to the young. And so we find, today, that even young architects and architecture students shrink back: more and more of them have sought alternatives to traditional architectural practice. After spending many years at difficult and prestigious schools preparing themselves for the correct professional procedures, some of them have, in fact, joined the opposition, working in so-called advocacy situations, assisting heretofore outnumbered and outmaneuvered community groups to resist the "projects" about to be foisted upon them by older generations of modern architects and planners.

121 Avianca Building, Bogota, Colombia, Monday, July 23, 1973. The fire in this 36-story building killed only four and injured only one hundred.

Seven months later, a fire in the Joelma Tower in São Paulo, Brazil, killed 179 and injured 300.

So the post-modern world is here, whether we like it or not. It was not invented by revisionist critics. It was spawned by the modern masters themselves, and by many of their failures. And now, what are the alternatives?

The first alternative to Modern Dogma should obviously be a moratorium on high-rise construction. It is outrageous that towers more than a hundred stories high are being built at a time when no honest engineer and no honest architect, anywhere on earth, can say *for certain* what these structures will do to the environment — in terms of monumental congestion of services (including roads and mass-transit lines), in terms of wind currents at sidewalk level, in terms of surrounding water tables, in terms of fire hazards, in terms of various sorts of interior traumata, in terms of despoiling the neighborhoods, in terms of visually polluting the skylines of our cities, and in terms of endangering the lives of those within or without, through conceivable structural and related failures.

No honest engineer or architect can honestly deny that these potential hazards exist — some remotely, others decidedly not — and that not nearly enough is really known about the ways extremely tall buildings will behave in response to high winds, in response to seismic tremors, or in response to any other fairly common quirk of nature. All we do know is that tall buildings (like a rather ungainly lump recently risen on State Street in downtown Boston) will cast an almost permanent shadow on such historic treasures as Faneuil Hall, and will probably further strangle traffic along what is jokingly referred to there as the Freedom Trail. All we do know is that these outrageous assaults upon our town- and cityscapes are launched for one reason only: to generate maximum profit for a handful of hit-and-run speculators who consider the surface of the earth their private preserve.

No other justification for the construction of supersky-scrapers exists today. And if that sole justification — avarice — is permitted to stand, then we must also permit hit-and-run speculators to poison our air for profit — just as we now, apparently, permit them to poison our land and our skylines for profit.

122 A serviceable, modern reinforced-concrete structure in West Berlin, being demolished (in 1976) to make way for urban bliss.

123 Low-rise, high-density community completed in Lima, Peru, in 1976. The densities are equal to those achieved in skyscraper housing projects, but the quality of life seems vastly superior.

122

123

124 Pedestrian street in the Lima community. This photograph was taken only a few weeks after the tenants had moved in; but the potential is clearly evident.

In Manhattan, housing projects have been built in recent years with densities of close to five hundred people per acre. (These density figures are imprecise because some cities work with "gross acreage" for their densities — they include a portion of the adjoining roads — and others do not.) Densities of such poisonous oppressiveness can be achieved only through the use of very high-rise towers, spaced cheek-by-jowl — and those densities are an abomination. In London, the authorities do not consider anything above two hundred people per acre decently acceptable, and they have found that this ratio can be achieved very comfortably by covering a site with humanly accessible low-rise, walk-up apartments and townhouses, clustered tightly along streets and around pleasant open spaces. The British architect Peter Land, who has done some of the most detailed and exhaustive research into low-rise, high-density, and expandable housing completed in the years since World War II, has written that "in contrast to the neighborhood as a vertical concept, the problem of the individual house on its own lot and its *multiplication into urban form* received . . . insufficient attention during the pioneering period of modern architecture. . . . The low-rise concept [is] a very viable and attractive alternative, if high densities can be achieved" (italics added). Peter Land then proceeded to demonstrate that densities of up to two hundred persons per acre could be achieved in urban situations using only two-story patio houses with individual gardens that are decidedly pleasant for families with (or without) children. Many housing officials refuse to believe this, but Land not only has his facts straight, he has actually built extremely high-density, low-rise housing in Lima, Peru, and knows whereof he speaks. One reason housing experts insist that one must go up, à la *Ville Radieuse*, to meet high-density needs is that the average density of New York City is only forty people per acre, but that includes quite a bit of open (and often useless) land.

124

There is no justification for skyscraper housing except, once again, avarice. Some population experts, like the British physicist J. H. Fremlin, have projected that if the earth's population continues to grow at its present rate, all of us will eventually have to be housed in a continuous megastructure, 2,000 stories tall, covering the entire globe. But Fremlin does not expect this to happen for another nine hundred years or so, by which time his prognosis may have been revised by intervening horrors, or by intervening sense. In any case, Fremlin won't be around to check on his prognosis — and neither will any of the rest of us.

125 Because of decentralization — via *Ville Radieuse,* or via Broadacre City — the superhighway has become the true determinant of modern, urban form.

126, 127, 128 Pruitt-Igoe public housing project, in St. Louis. Built in the 1950s and hailed as a truly enlightened scheme, it had to be dynamited, at least in part, less than twenty years later. Reason: it had proved to be totally destructive of human life, and a menace to the few remaining survivors.

The second alternative to Modern Dogma should be a moratorium on the wholesale destruction of existing buildings, historic landmarks as well as corner drugstores (which may, of course, qualify as the former). The population of the earth doubled between 1930 and 1975; to destroy any building, except under very special conditions of emergency, is therefore a crime against humanity, past, present, and future. The destruction of hundreds of thousands of perfectly serviceable structures to make way for some hypothetical future ''development'' has generated more vacant sites, and more dismal but profitable parking lots, in most U.S. cities than may have been generated in Europe by the bombing raids of World War II. In New York City, as I write, some 30,000 dwelling units (most of them low-income) are lost annually to demolition (and other forms of vandalism), while fewer than 5,000 units a year (most of these luxurious) are being added to the city's housing stock. For the past five or ten years — ever since 1970 or thereabouts — the cost of new construction around the world has become so exorbitant that it is now quite feasible, in economic terms, to reuse old and dilapidated buildings that were once believed to be too uneconomical to recycle.

In any event, the only true justification for the demolition of a perfectly serviceable older structure is, once again, avarice. It is not an admissible justification in a time of desperate human need.

125

The third alternative to Modern Dogma should be a moratorium on the construction of all new highways, certainly in all developed nations. Between 1930 and 1960, the length of paved intercity highways in the United States increased from about 100,000 miles to more than 400,000 miles. And between 1960 and 1975, the length of paved intercity highways then proceeded to double, whereupon a nation built almost entirely upon the conspicuous waste of gasoline (and of aluminum, rubber, steel, plastic, and glass) proceeded to grind to a halt.

The vast highway building program in the United States meant not only that the cement industry and its many constituents grew very rich; it also meant that decentralization was dramatically increased, and that suburban sprawl was given a huge boost. The profits generated for homebuilders and their suppliers were staggering — and the destruction of the American city, and its life, and its form, was almost total.

Decentralization into suburbia via the superhighway did not merely drain our cities of people and of revenues; it also set up a lethal confrontation between our inner cities and their suburbs. Modern planners are fond of talking about huge, homogeneous inkblots on our national maps that are supposed to represent ''megalopoles'' of impressive size — 20 to 30 million bodies each. And the assumption is that these jolly inkblots would act in unison, politically, economically, and socially. Alas, nothing of the sort has happened. Suburbs have become increasingly white and middle-class; cities, the reverse. Interaction does exist — at sword's point; cooperation does not. An enormously expensive highway building program, costing at least $100 billion between the early 1950s and 1975 alone, has helped to decentralize and then to antagonize. The program, as Schumacher puts it, has made people ''footloose'' — and thus polarized them.

It may be too late to reverse the trend, but it is not too late to discourage further decentralization. A moratorium on highway construction will, at least, encourage people to reexamine (or re-create) whatever charms are left in our cities. A moratorium on highway construction within the confines of our cities will, at least, put an end to the further amputation of neighborhoods from one another.

26

27

28

The fourth alternative to Modern Dogma is legislation to hold our building industries responsible for the performance of their products. Very few laws exist today to protect the public from the potentially lethal impact of untested but highly touted building products — and any modern architect credulous enough to specify a product "guaranteed" by its manufacturer to perform miracles may find himself or herself involved in interminable law suits when the product fails to live up to its guarantees. Until the building industries are strictly policed and held accountable for performance standards at least as rigid as those imposed on the manufacturers of automobiles and pharmaceuticals, most modern buildings may prove to be hazardous to your health, and to mine.

This is hardly an exaggeration. In 1974, to cite one example, Yale University discovered that a sprayed-on asbestos coating applied to the concrete ceilings of the university's School of Art and Architecture in order to soundproof the spaces beneath was also shedding exceedingly unhealthy asbestos fibers that were promptly inhaled by the university's wards. The manufacturer of this lethal product, having gone out of business, left the problem in the laps of the architect and his client. The architect was threatened with lawsuits; the client evacuated the building and began to refurbish all of the ceilings. The victims — the students and faculty long exposed to agents believed to cause lung cancer — had virtually no recourse.

Another, much more dramatic example is the flash fire that destroyed the Buckminster Fuller–designed geodesic dome in Montreal on May 20, 1976. The huge dome, framed in steel and clad in acrylic, was built to house the U.S. exhibit at Expo '67. During that World's Fair, the beautiful structure usually held anywhere from 5,000 to 10,000 visitors at any given time. The acrylic was treated with a fire-retardant, but apparently it wasn't up to snuff; a welder's torch inadvertently ignited the entire structure in a matter of minutes, turning the huge bubble into a mass of liquid acrylic (and blackened steel) before the fire engines could reach the scene. Happily, only one person was unaccounted for; had this happened during Expo '67, the toll might have been twenty to forty times that suffered in the 1871 Chicago fire. (Fuller, a most humane man who trusts technology, has long advocated enclosing entire cities with plastic-clad geodesic domes.) Does anyone truly believe that our building industries should be free to endanger human life?

Or even to soil the environment? Another highly advertised product — a so-called self-oxidizing steel, a material that will rust up to a point and then acquire a handsome patina, and that will then, supposedly, stop rusting after about two years, and continue to flaunt that patina until hell freezes over — is a fine case in point. What the rust manufacturers forgot to mention is that their stuff may also indelibly stain most other surfaces and materials within its reach; and that the rusty dust blowing off a "self-oxidizing" building will discolor the grounds adjacent to it. This is precisely analogous to permitting a power plant to deposit layers of soot upon its neighbors' properties. It isn't done — or, if it is, the neighbors go to court.

There are innumerable building products in common use today that are a potential menace to users and innocent bystanders alike. Many of the foam plastics routinely used as insulation in partitions or as upholstery in furniture will generate poisonous fumes in case of fire, so that even a minor conflagration can quickly produce fatalities. Heat-activated elevator buttons, another blessing of advanced building technology, were outlawed in a number of American cities, but only after several people had died in fires when they were trapped in New York elevators. And no dependable research is available, to date, to document the effect upon the eyesight of American office workers of the staggering "foot-candle" standards at desk levels decreed (not surprisingly) by the manufacturers of lighting fixtures and light bulbs. Consumer protection also seems long overdue in that particular area of modern living.

The list of irresponsible offenders is almost endless. For years, it has been a common urban experience to have sheets of plate glass pop out of their neoprene gaskets and come sailing down the avenue in search of a pedestrian neck any time wind velocities exceeded what the neoprene manufacturers considered admissible. Building codes are supposed to prevent inadvertent decapitations and, theoretically and actually, architects are held responsible for the performance of the products they specify. No architect can possibly test a complex product in his drafting room, or an assemblage of complex products — any more than a doctor can maintain a pharmaceutical research institute in his closet or a policeman can operate a ballistics lab in his garage. Only the manufacturers of all these blessings are properly equipped to test their products before marketing them, and they have seemed rather lackadaisical in that pursuit.

129, 130 Park and Sixth Avenues, respectively, in Manhattan, zoned for business. "No there, there," as Gertrude Stein said.

Although the building industries of the developed nations are by and large irresponsible in their promotion of untested products, it is clear that the specifications for many of those products were initially written by the Modern Movement itself; manufacturers simply tried to fill the bill. As noted earlier, Mies van der Rohe had said, in 1924, that "our first consideration must be to find a new building material. . . . Then the new architecture will come into its own." Well, our building industries have found plenty of new building materials, but a great many of them have sabotaged the new architecture and destroyed much of its credibility.

129

The fifth alternative to Modern Dogma must be a moratorium on zoning — that dimwitted notion that has turned so many of our cities into lopsided raisin cakes, as Henry Hope Reed once put it, with the raisins in one place and the cake in the other. Or, to be more precise, a moratorium on *single-use* zoning: the idea that a city is an assemblage of ghettos — residential, industrial, commercial, cultural, educational, governmental, or, for that matter, pornographic.

In the United States and elsewhere, most major cities have been zoned by elaborate legislation. Houston, Texas, has not, and it seems no worse but also no better than New York, which has been most heavily zoned. In fact, Boston, which is rather backward in the eyes of zoning experts, seems considerably more interesting than Manhattan, which has won accolades from the aficionados of zoning. And Isfahan, that most wonderful of all cities, has never even heard of zoning; its inhabitants work where they live, and shop where they work, and pray where they play, and entertain where they work. Single-use zoning — a notion most seriously advanced by the pioneers of the Modern Movement — is, quite simply, the end of urban civilization.

130

131 Diagram for a perfectly zoned, ideal modern city, done in the 1920s.

131

The sixth alternative to Modern Dogma is to scale down the gigantic plans hitherto advocated (and very rarely implemented) and to plan on a humanly comprehensible scale — or, as Schumacher suggests, not at all!

Our libraries on architectural and planning theory are bursting with "planning studies" that usually begin with a Mercator projection of the globe, then zero in on the United States, then Pennsylvania (say), then Philadelphia, then downtown Philadelphia, and then, finally, upon one block on the west side of Rittenhouse Square. The idea is to convey global intentions; the fact, however, is that nobody is fooled: the intentions — and the attainable targets — are quite local.

And this is just as well. In a democratic society, plans must inevitably be scaled to the size of neighborhoods, because there, happily, is where the voters make their decisions. But, just as important, it is only on that sort of scale that post-modern architects are capable of functioning. Not many superplanners since Georges Eugène Haussmann or Albert Speer have had the authority "to stir men's blood" by bulldozing their neighborhoods. Those who have done so in recent years, without explicit authorization, have been dramatically discredited.

Even modern planners now admit that "little plans" are probably preferable to big ones; not only can they be implemented more easily, but they often help generate a spontaneous, natural development or growth that is much more responsive to people's needs than Burnham's "noble, logical diagram." Very often, when a single city block is closed to vehicular traffic, the result is not merely to reroute peripheral traffic, but also to generate a new neighborhood focus, which then, in turn, may generate other urban events a block or two or five away from the original planning decision. The trick, of course, is to

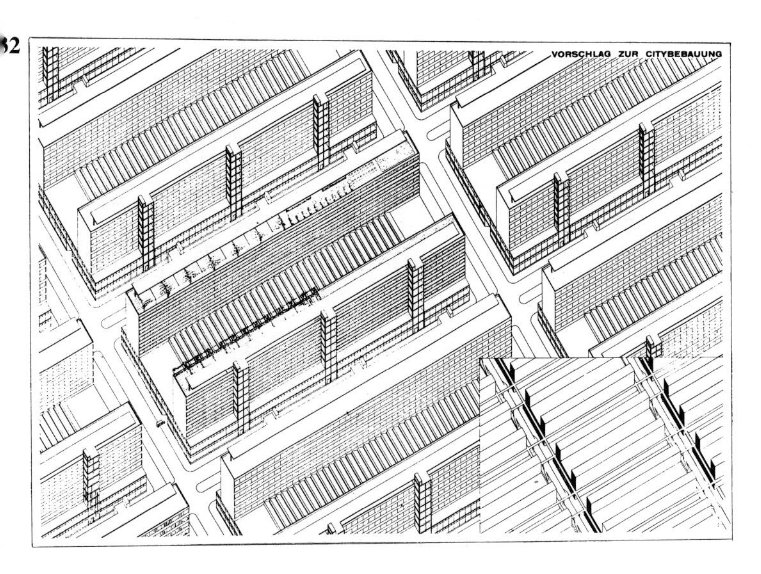

132 Bird's-eye view of another "Ideal City." No people are in sight, and none are expected.

identify the most promising points of impact where planning initiative is likely to trigger the most positive results.

Such planning initiatives require a great deal of subtlety; sometimes the preservation of a single building, or the widening of a sidewalk, or the "incentive" payoff to a single developer will start a chain reaction that can transform an entire neighborhood, and conceivably an entire town. In Boston, the bulldozing of the former West End, and the erection upon its mass grave of the master-planned Charles River Park, did precisely nothing desirable for the city; but the subtle revitalization of Boston's old harbor wharves, which involved no bulldozing at all, is generating a truly organic urban renewal.

Planners in most other major cities in the United States and elsewhere are discovering to their surprise and delight that "little plans" are infinitely more interesting than "big plans." They are also somewhat more readily implementable, given the facts of life in a participatory democracy.

The seventh alternative to Modern Dogma should be a radical restructuring of architectural education. Over the past thirty or forty years, schools of architecture in most developed or developing countries have shifted their focus from the training of specialists in building and design to the training of generalists in some vaguely defined areas of "living."

Initially, Walter Gropius, at the Bauhaus in Germany and later at Harvard, had preached that architecture would become increasingly the product of "teamwork" — a reasonable prognosis, though there is not much evidence in the past or the present that great buildings are likely to be created by teams (and there is much evidence, as suggested earlier, that committees charged with the design of a horse are likely to come up with the shape of a camel). Still, there is no question that the design of a building or a building project today requires input from men and women of many different disciplines: essential experts such as mechanical, structural, and other engineers; consultants in many special fields, from landscaping to acoustics; and still more specialized consultants in peripheral areas such as economics, psychology, anthropology, and whatnot.

But Gropius's vision of architecture as the product of teamwork suggested that the architect must be the coordinator of all these bits and pieces of advice, that the architect must ultimately accept and reject and make decisive judgments that would shape the final product. Many educators who tried to emulate Gropius misunderstood that essential point, and proceeded to inundate their students with elaborate courses in everything from group dynamics to marriage counseling — forgetting that the very idea of teamwork suggested that such invaluable bits and pieces of advice would be contributed by outside consultants, not necessarily by the architect ultimately responsible for the building. These educational theorists began to overload the curricula of architectural schools with such mountains of extraneous and largely superfluous "information" that students were able to graduate from certain famous schools without ever having been taught how to build or even to draw anything at all — and without ever having been taught how to proceed from the nuts-and-bolts knowledge of building to the judgmental speculation of design.

One reason for this educational chaos was, quite clearly, the fact that most teachers of architecture, at least in the United States, did not really know from personal experience how buildings were put together, and so they took refuge in obscure and muddled pursuits of peripheral disciplines (about which, most of the time, they knew even less). They spoke increasingly about such things as "the social obligation" of architects, not knowing (in part because the Modern Movement considered history "bunk") that the social obligation of an architect is perhaps to produce buildings of quality, and that it is, further, to make certain that the buildings in question will stand up rather than fall down.

Few students in the past two or three decades have been taught how to produce or even appreciate works of art (possibly an unteachable expertise, but one worth a certain degree of effort); few students have been taught how to build buildings that will not collapse. But many have been exposed to vast insights having to do with social psychology, environmental engineering, conceptual speculation, and other protoplasmic disciplines that usually defy clear definition.

It is unlikely that Gropius wanted architectural education to take its present diffuse and imprecise form. But the jargon of the Modern Movement, to which most of the modern masters contributed volubly, had a great deal to do with shaping its educational structure. The system developed by the traditional École des Beaux-Arts in Paris was tossed out — and with it went architectural history and the concept of architecture as an applied art. To take the place of these traditional concepts came functionalism (alleged), economy (alleged), technology (alleged), social justice (alleged), health (alleged), happiness (alleged). These noble objectives were touted as the principal justifications of modern architecture, and so, the schools that sprang up to teach modern architecture began to overflow with efficiency experts, management consultants, sociologists, economists, psychologists, and most of all with educationists, i.e., people interested not in what they were supposed to teach, but in educational methodology and educational politics. (This is roughly analogous to a liberal government whose reform-minded office holders become more interested in tax collection than in whatever they were elected to reform in the first place.)

A mere two dozen years after the Beaux-Arts system was overthrown in most of the modern world, schools of architecture had become more massively bureaucratized and politicized than the old École had ever been. (One reason for the popularity of playing politics at these schools, according to one observer, is that the stakes are so small!) The new, modern schools produced a steady stream of more or less pompous generalists and an occasional tiny trickle of people who actually knew how to draw, how to build, how to design, and how, once in a lifetime perhaps, to produce a building that might qualify as a work of art.

And finally, there may have to be a moratorium on architecture itself. The Modern Movement is close to a hundred years old, depending upon when you want to start counting. It has had its heroic moments: Wright's Robie House, his Unity Temple, his Taliesin East and West, and much, much more; Mies van der Rohe's Barcelona Pavilion, his Crown Hall at Illinois Tech, his New National Gallery in West Berlin, and also much, much more; Le Corbusier's Villa Savoye, his Unité d'Habitation at Marseilles, his great palaces at Chandigarh. And there have been truly inspired works by many others, from Alvar Aalto — that gentle humanist who never subscribed to the dogmatic creed and who preferred to say about his work only that "I build" — to I. M. Pei and Harry Cobb — whose razor-edged and mirrored prism, the John Hancock Tower in Boston, is (despite all of its grotesque problems) the most dazzling work of minimal sculpture produced in this century to date (and certainly the largest): a mirror held up to the clouds.

It has been a truly fantastic period in the history of architecture in more ways than one; protesting its faith in reason, the movement was, in fact, the most irrational since King Ludwig of Bavaria went mildly berserk. Protesting its faith in the common man and in an egalitarian world, it wiped out "little people" right and left, and their neighborhoods, in the service of private or state capitalism. Protesting its utter devotion to advanced technology, it juggled building materials and methods with the insouciance of the most adroit circus clown. And protesting its total dedication to the city as the one and only seat and source and mainspring of civilization, it rendered the city unmanageable and, in effect, scattered its inhabitants to the winds.

No period in the recorded history of architecture has been more creative, or more destructive, or more exhausting for all concerned — architects as well as innocent bystanders. It is time to take a break. Whether one likes it or not, very little "architecture" in the accepted sense is going to be commissioned or built for some time to come. The reasons are clear enough.

First, an increasingly egalitarian world does not have very much use for what appears to it to be an aristocratic art.

Second, a profession that has failed to come to grips with the central issues of our time — the issues created by the so-called population bomb — may have disqualified itself from serious consideration. When the director of some outfit called the Institute for Architecture and Urban Studies (an offshoot of New York's Museum of Modern Art) can tell his students to "leave reality out of it" — "it" being their work in architecture and urban studies — when that appears to represent the dominant view of at least *one* significant segment of his profession; well, then the real world will be quick to return the compliment, and leave architecture out of *its* plans, and render architects the world over massively unemployed.

And finally, there will be a moratorium on architecture because clients of architecture seem, today, to lack the inclination to build Great Works of Art. Several years ago Sir Nikolaus Pevsner, the British architectural historian, said that an important reason for the decline in the quality of our architecture was the decline in the quality of contemporary clients. Unlike the aristocratic clients of earlier centuries, Pevsner suggested, today's clients were, by and large, visually and otherwise illiterate, and demanded very little from their architects other than low cost and high efficiency.

Quite true, and quite understandable. In a world whose population has more than quadrupled since the birth of Louis Sullivan, problems of architectural quality are likely to be less pressing than problems of building quantity. When the architectural elite in the developed nations (and in some of the developing ones) rededicates itself, as it has been doing periodically, to the concept of architecture as an abstract, even unbuildable (and certainly unreal) art, it is telling the rest of the world to go and eat cake. And the rest of the world does not think this is a frightfully funny joke.

And when the left wing of that same architectural elite, often identified with such odd places as the School of Environmental Design at Berkeley, California, operates its educational establishments to turn out graduates who may not necessarily know how to build, but who do know how to raise somebody's diminishing consciousness inside an inflatable cocoon — well, then the real world is merely confirmed in its "instinctive guess" that the architectural profession has gone collectively mad. At one extreme are the designers of unbuildable buildings, at the other extreme are the designers of buildable nonbuildings; somewhere in the middle, in the geographic center, roughly, of the real world, there is a great big void, ignored, it seems, by most architects of talent.

So the worldwide moratorium on modern architecture was decreed not by some venal outside forces, but by the curious elites that have come to dominate the architectural scene. The moratorium will continue until there is a rapprochement between architecture and reality. And out of that rapprochement may come a situation in which the *applied art of architecture* can be resurrected and made again part of the human experience from which the Modern Movement seems to have divorced it.

It is, quite simply, that after a run of a hundred years or so Modern Dogma is worn out. It has had its days, and some of these days were indeed glorious. There are no reasons for regret; the Renaissance gave way to Mannerism, and that to the bombast of the Baroque, and that, in turn, to sugary Rococo. We are now close to the end of one epoch, and well before the start of a new one. During this period of transition there will be no moratorium on building, and for obvious reasons. There will just be more and more architecture without architects. Too bad for the practitioners of architecture, present company included. But hardly a mortal blow to the quality of the man-made environment; there is no evidence whatsoever that recent architecture with architects is, in fact, superior to architecture without; or that it generates more bliss.

Out of this period of nonarchitecture there may emerge a new direction, a direction based on shared ideals and shared realities. An architecture, as E. F. Schumacher might have put it, "as if people mattered." And an architecture as if the real world mattered: the real world's hardware, the real world's true resources (human as well as material), the real world's aspirations. Ortega y Gasset once wrote that "order is not a pressure which is imposed on society from without, but an equilibrium which is set up from within." Neither is architecture, and the new architecture will not come into its own until there is "an equilibrium set up from within," a body of shared aspirations. Only then, I think, will we fashion a new landscape of vision, of utility, and of art.

When the Modern Movement came to the fore, it professed, as we have seen, certain shared ideals: devotion to a sort of democratic collectivism, industrialization and machine aesthetic, devotion to the city, and devotion to the future. It was a good try, and it will continue to move a great many of us, if only to nostalgia.

But this is the moment of truth, for me and for many of us who are modern architects. We have seen and lived this future, and it just simply doesn't work. The Modern Movement — the creed in which we were raised and to which we pledged allegiance throughout our professional lives — has reached the end of the road.

BIOSPHERE

Postscript

Many of the technical data referred to in this book were gathered over a period of a dozen years or so, while I served as the Editor-in-Chief of the *Architectural Forum* and, after that, of *Architecture Plus*. The issues of those two late, lamented publications between, roughly, 1963 and 1975 contain much of the background material on which this book is based.

There are many other sources, including a few that are not as well known as they ought to be. I should like to single out these: the November 19, 1975, issue of the British publication, the *Architects' Journal,* which was devoted in major part to the subject of professional "Incompetence"; a chilling booklet entitled *Fires in High-Rise Buildings* published in 1974 by the National Fire Protection Association; the various essays and reports published by (and about the work of) the British architect and expert on high-density, low-rise housing, Peter Land (most specifically one in the May 1976 issue of *Harvard Magazine*); a report on the utilization of research results in the building industry published in June 1974 by Duncan M. Wilson of the Boston Architectural Center, under a grant from the National Science Foundation; the writings of my friend and one-time associate, Jane Jacobs, and those of Lewis Mumford; the pages of the *Journal of Architectural Research,* published jointly by the Royal Institute of British Architects and the American Institute of Architects; and the issues, over the past twenty-five years or so, of all the architectural (and related professional) publications which I have devoured with sometimes flagging interest and often increasing gloom: the British *Architectural Review*; the Italian *Casabella, Domus, L'Architettura* and *Controspazio*; the German *Bauwelt* and *Bauen + Wohnen*; the Austrian publication *Transparent*; the Swiss publication *Werk*; the Japanese architectural magazines that bedazzle us in growing numbers, with lovely illustrations accompanied by utterly incomprehensible prose — especially that gem, *A + U* (Architecture + Urbanism); and many, many more, including innumerable irreverent and usually short-lived periodicals published by students at schools of architecture in the United States and elsewhere.

Needless to say, none of the above has endorsed any of the views expressed in this book; indeed, some of those publications have served primarily to supply me — unwittingly — with the ammunition needed to demolish the targets at hand.

The most intangible sources for this book must, I regret, be taken on faith by the reader:

They are, first of all, a body of experience in building in the real world. I do not pretend that I have built anywhere near as much as others of my generation (I have been too busy writing, editing, and teaching); but I have built enough to know that most of the articles of faith that I once held, most religiously, most devoutly, simply did not measure up to the test of time, to the test of function, or to the test of service to the human race and its condition. How would I know? Because, like any other architect, like any other writer, I have had my eyes, ears, nose and several other fairly perceptive organs (including my head) examined, and their perceptions sharpened at the various schools of architecture I attended, and since.

33 Montreal, May 20, 1976. The U.S. Pavilion at Expo '67 was a beautiful dream, but modern technology, it seems, wasn't quite up to snuff.

A second source of information, most heavily drawn upon in the writing of this book, is also most difficult to quantify or to evaluate for accuracy. And that is the seemingly interminable talk that goes on among fellow architects.

Unlike doctors and lawyers, who seem amongst themselves to talk primarily about making money, architects (when thrown together) talk almost exclusively about what went wrong, where, how, when and through whose fault. (They also, sometimes, talk about what went right — but the opportunities to do so seem to be dwindling.) Like all my fellow architects, I have spent years in talking about our common problems — often off-the-record, because so many of them perceived me, primarily, as a journalist. So this source, also, must be taken on faith.

I should, perhaps, mention one additional fact. Unlike most of my fellow architects, I have long lived and worked in modern buildings: I have lived in two houses of my own design, and in two apartment buildings that were designed by architects of high repute whom I admire. I have worked in two of the outstanding structures in Rockefeller Center, in Manhattan, and now work in a building in Boston that was the winning entry in a nationwide competition. I have been my own pet guinea pig, and the experience has been very interesting.

Credits

1. Architects: Ulrich Franzen & Associates. Photo: George Cserna.

2. Architect: Paul Rudolph. Drawing: Courtesy Paul Rudolph.

3. Architect: Paul Rudolph. Photo: Roy Berkeley.

4. Architects: Stewart, Noble, Class & Partners (new building); Furness Evans & Company (1890 building). Photo: author.

5. Architects: Cochran, Stephenson & Donkervoet. Photo: George Cserna.

6. Architects and Engineers: Arup Associates. Photo: John Donat.

7. Architect: Giorgio Cavaglieri. Photo: Marc Neuhof.

8. Architect: Giorgio Cavaglieri. Photo: George Cserna.

9. Architect: Graham Gund. Photo: Steve Rosenthal.

10. Architects: B.B.P.R. Photo: Paolo Monti.

11. Architects: B.B.P.R. Photo: "Fotogramma."

12. Architects: B.B.P.R. Photo: Paolo Monti.

13. Architects: Kallmann & McKinnell. Drawing: Courtesy Kallmann & McKinnell.

14. Architect: Shin Takaya. Photo: Rene Burri.

15. Architect: L. Mies van der Rohe. Drawing: Courtesy The Museum of Modern Art, New York.

16. Photo: Norman F. Carver, Jr.

17. Architect: L. Mies van der Rohe. Photo: author.

18. Drawing: Courtesy Foster Associates.

19. Artist: Constantin Brancusi. Photo: Courtesy The Museum of Modern Art, New York.

20. Photo: author.

21. Photo: author.

22. Photo: author.

23. Photo: author.

24. Architect: Le Corbusier. Photo: author.

25. Architect: Le Corbusier. Photo: author.

26. Architect: Le Corbusier. Photo: author.

27. Architect: Le Corbusier. Photo: author.

28. Photo: author.

29. Architect: Ulrich Franzen & Associates. Photo: George Cserna.

30. Photo: Fototeca Servizio Informazioni.

31. Architect: F. E. Graef. Photo: author.

32. Architect: John Correja. Photo: author.

33. Architect: Moshe Safdie. Photo: author.

34. Architect: Moshe Safdie. Photo: author.

35. Drawing: Courtesy SCSD.

36. Architects: Baker & Blake (Peter Blake, Partner-in-Charge). Photo: Norman McGrath.

37. Photo: Martin Pawley.

38. Photo: Martin Pawley.

39. Drawing: Courtesy General Panel System.

40. Drawing: Courtesy General Panel System.

41. Drawing: Courtesy General Panel System.

42. Drawing: Courtesy General Panel System.

43. Photo: Courtesy U.S. Steel.

44. Photo: author.

45. Architects: Harrison & Abramovitz; and Skidmore, Owings & Merrill. Photo: author.

46. Photo: author.

47. Drawing: Courtesy *Oeuvre Complète*.

48. Photo: author.

49. Photo: author.

50. Photo: Courtesy *The Architectural Forum*.

51. Drawing: Saul Steinberg.

52. Photo: Peter Vanderwarker.

53. Photo: author.

54. Photo: Kevin Cole (*Boston Herald American*).

55. Photo: Kevin Cole (*Boston Herald American*).

56. Architects: Alison and Peter Smithson. Photo: Sandra Lousada.

57. Photo: author.

58. Photo: author.

59. Photo: Milan Pavić.

60. Photo: Courtesy Turistkomerc-Zagreb.

61. Photo: S. Radovcic.

62. Photo: Daniela Lusin.

63. Drawing: Courtesy *Oeuvre Complète*.

64. Photo: author.

65. Photo: Clemens Kalischer.

66. Photo: author.

67. Photo: author.

68. Photo: author.

69. Photo: author.

70. Photo: author.

71. Photo: Frank Tolopko.

72. Photo: author.

73. Drawing: Courtesy *Oeuvre Complète*.

74. Photo: author.

75. Photo: author.

76. Photo: author.

77. Drawing: Courtesy *Oeuvre Complète*.

78. Design: François Dallegret.

79. Design: Ron Herron.

80. Drawing: Courtesy Rockefeller Center, New York.

81. Photo: author.

82. Drawing: Courtesy *Oeuvre Complète*.

83. Drawing: Courtesy Thomas Sharp.

84. Drawing: Courtesy *Oeuvre Complète*.

85. Drawing: Courtesy *The Ideal Communist City*.

86. Photo: author.

87. Photo: author.

88. Photo: Courtesy *The Architectural Forum*.

89. Photo: author.

90. Photo: author.

91. Architect: Sir Edwin Lutyens. Photo: author.

92. Architect: Sir Edwin Lutyens. Photo: author.

93. Photo: author.

94. Photo: author.

95. Photo: author.

96. Architects: Skidmore, Owings & Merrill. Photo: author.

97. Architect: Marcel Breuer. Drawing: Courtesy The Museum of Modern Art, New York.

98. Photo: Milan Pavić.

99. Photo: author.

100. Architect: Giancarlo De Carlo. Photo: author.

101. Photo: author.

102. Photo: author.

103. Photo: author.

104. Architects: Keyes, Lethbridge & Condon. Photo: author.

105. Architects: Wilhelm Piedje and Josef Lehmbruck. Photo: Gottfried Planck.

106. Designer: Gerrit Rietveld. Photo: Clement Meadmore.

107. Designer: Frank Lloyd Wright. Photo: Herman Kroll.

108. Designers of steel chairs: Le Corbusier and Charlotte Perriand. Photo: author.

109. Designer: Verner Panton. Drawing: Courtesy *The Modern Chair*.

110. Designer: Gerrit Rietveld. Photo: Courtesy The Museum of Modern Art, New York.

111. Designer: Gerrit Rietveld. Photo: Clement Meadmore.

112. Designer: Vladimir Tatlin. Photo: Clement Meadmore.

113. Designer: Gerrit Rietveld. Drawing: Courtesy *The Modern Chair*.

114. Designer: Gerrit Rietveld. Photo: Courtesy The Museum of Modern Art, New York.

115. Designer: Marianne Brandt. Photo: Courtesy The Museum of Modern Art, New York.

116. Designer: Ole Mathiesen. Photo: Stephen H. Lewis.

117. Designer: Charles O. Perry. Photo: author.

118. Photo: Courtesy *The Architectural Forum*.

119. Architects: Oscar Niemeyer et al. Photo: Charles Correa.

120. Architects: Oscar Niemeyer et al. Photo: Charles Correa.

121. Photo: Courtesy *Fires in High-Rise Buildings*.

122. Photo: author.

123. Executive architect-in-charge: Peter Land. Photo: Peter Land.

124. Executive architect-in-charge: Peter Land. Photo: Peter Land.

125. Photo: author.

126. Photo: Courtesy *The St. Louis Post Dispatch*.

127. Photo: Courtesy *The St. Louis Post Dispatch*.

128. Photo: Courtesy *The St. Louis Post Dispatch*.

129. Photo: author.

130. Photo: author.

131. Architect: Ludwig Hilberseimer. Drawing: Courtesy The Museum of Modern Art, New York.

132. Architect: Ludwig Hilberseimer. Drawing: Courtesy *Contemporary Architecture*.

133. Architect: R. Buckminster Fuller. Photo: Doug Lehman (The Group Productions Ltd.).